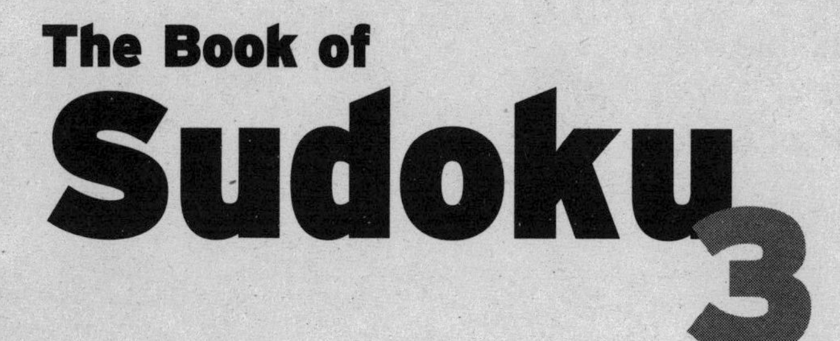
The Book of
Sudoku 3

Also Available
The Book of Sudoku #1
The Book of Sudoku #2

The Book of Sudoku 3

Compiled by Michael Mepham

THE OVERLOOK PRESS
WOODSTOCK & NEW YORK

This edition first published in paperback in the United States in 2005 by
The Overlook Press, Peter Mayer Publishers, Inc.
New York & Woodstock

New York:
141 Wooster Street
New York, NY 10012

Woodstock:
One Overlook Drive
Woodstock, NY 12498
www.overlookpress.com
[for individual orders, bulk and special sales, contact our Woodstock office]

Cataloging-in-Publication Data is available from the Library of Congress

Manufactured in the United States of America
ISBN 1-58567-783-3
9 8 7 6 5 4 3 2

Contents

Solution to the sudoku on the cover

8	4	1	6	9	3	5	2	7
6	7	5	2	1	4	9	8	3
9	3	2	5	8	7	1	4	6
3	8	4	1	5	9	6	7	2
7	1	6	3	2	8	4	9	5
5	2	9	4	7	6	3	1	8
4	5	7	9	3	2	8	6	1
1	9	8	7	6	5	2	3	4
2	6	3	8	4	1	7	5	9

Solving Sudoku

What is sudoku?

You would imagine that with such a name this puzzle originated in Japan, but it has been around for many years in the UK. However, the Japanese found an example under the title 'Number Place' in an American magazine and translated it as something quite different: su meaning number; doku which translates as single or bachelor. It immediately caught on in Japan, where number puzzles are much more prevalent than word puzzles. Crosswords don't work well in the Japanese language.

The sudoku puzzle reached craze status in Japan in 2004 and the craze spread to the UK through the puzzle pages of national newspapers. *The Daily Telegraph* uses the name Sudoku, but you may see it called su doku elsewhere. However, there is no doubt that the word has been adopted into modern parlance, much like 'crossword'.

Sudoku is not a mathematical or arithmetical puzzle. It works just as well if the numbers are substituted with letters or some other symbols, but numbers work best.

				8	3	4		
3					4	8	2	1
7								
		9	4		1		8	3
4	6		5		7	1		
								7
1	2	5	3					9
		7	2	4				

The challenge

Here is an unsolved sudoku puzzle. It consists of a 9x9 grid that has been subdivided into 9 smaller grids of 3x3 squares. Each puzzle has a logical and unique solution. **To solve the puzzle, each row, column and box must contain each of the numbers 1 to 9.**

Throughout this book I refer to the whole puzzle as the **grid**, a small 3x3 grid as a **box** and the cell that contains the number as a **square**.

Rows and columns are referred to with row number first, followed by the column number: 4,5 is row 4, column 5; 2,8 is row 2, column 8. Boxes are numbered 1–9 in reading order, i.e. 123, 456, 789.

About guessing

Try not to. Until you have progressed to the tough and diabolical puzzles, guessing is not only totally unnecessary, but will lead you up paths that can make the puzzle virtually unsolvable. Simple logic is all that is required for gentle and moderate puzzles. Of the 132 puzzles in this book only the last 34 will require deep analysis, and that is dealt with later on in this introduction.

Making a start

1

To solve sudoku puzzles you will use logic. You will ask yourself questions like: '**if** a 1 is in this box, will it go in this column?' or '**if** a 9 is already in this row, can a 9 go in this square?'

				8	3	4		
3					4	8	2	1
7								
		9	4		1		8	3
4	6		5		7	1		
								7
1	2	5	3					9
		7	2	4				8

To make a start, look at each of the boxes and see which squares are empty, at the same time checking that square's column and row for a missing number.

In this example, look at box 9. There is no 8 in the box, but there is an 8 in column 7 and in column 8. The only place for an 8 is in column 9, and in this box the only square available is in row 9. So put an 8 in that square. **You have solved your first number.**

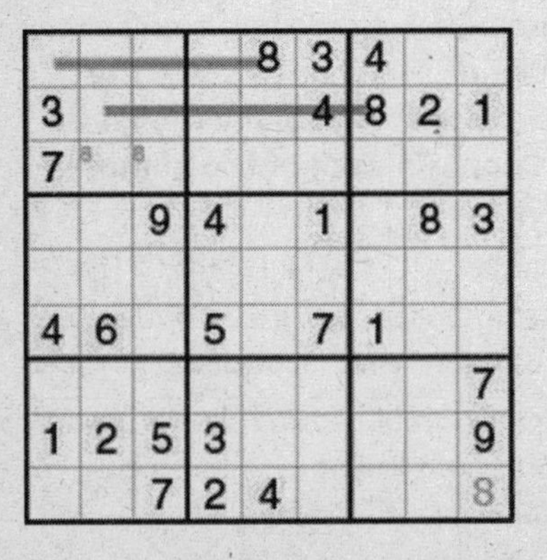

2

Continuing to think about 8, there is no 8 in box 1, but you can see an 8 in rows 1 and 2. So, in box 1, an 8 can only go in row 3, but there are 2 squares available. Make a note of this by pencilling in a small 8 in both squares. Later, when we have found the position of the 8 in boxes 4 or 7 we will be able to disprove one of our 8s in box 1.

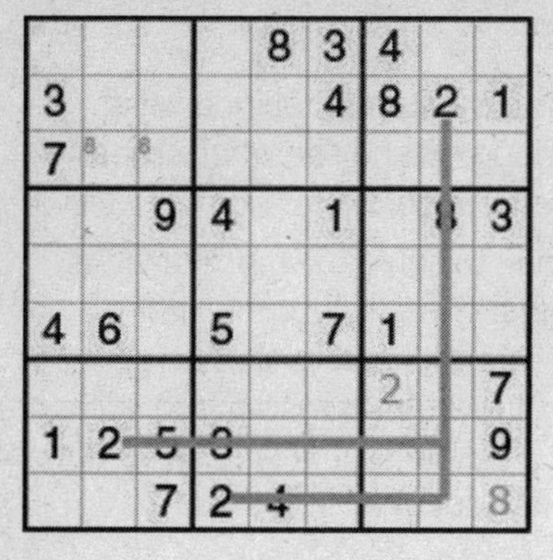

3

We were looking at box 9. As you can see, there is a 2 in boxes 7 and 8, but none in box 9. The 2s in row 8 and row 9 mean the only place for a 2 in box 9 appears to be in row 7, and as there is already a 2 in column 8, there is only one square left in that box for a 2 to go. You can enter the 2 for box 9 at 7,7.

				8	3	4		
3					4	8	2	1
7	8	8						
		9	4		1		8	3
							4	4
4	6		5		7	1		
						2		7
1	2	5	3					9
		7	2	4				8

4

There is a similar situation with the 4s in boxes 4 and 5, but here the outcome is not so definite. Together with the 4 in column 7 these 4s eliminate all the available squares in box 6 apart from two. Pencil a small 4 in these two squares. Later on, one or other of your pencil marks will be proved or disproved.

				8	3	4		
3					4	8	2	1
7	8	8						
		9	4		1		8	3
							4	24
4	6		5		7	1		2
						2		7
1	2	5	3					9
		7	2	4				8

5

Having proved the 2 in box 9 earlier, check to see if this helps you to solve anything else. For example, the 2 in box 3 shows where the 2 should go in box 6: it can only go in column 9, where there are two available squares. As we have not yet proved the position of the 4, one of the squares may be either a 4 or a 2.

				8	3	4		
3					4	8	2	1
7	8	8						
		9	4		1		8	3
							4	24
4	6		5		7	1		2
						2		7
1	2	5	3					9
		7	2	4				8

6

Now solve a number on your own. Look at box 8 and see where the number 7 should go.

Continue to solve the more obvious numbers. There will come a point when you will need to change your strategy. What follows will provide you with some schemes to solve the complete sudoku.

The search for the lone number

		3	5	678	4	1		
	7			2			5	
5	2			178			6	
		8	6	5	9	3		
	3		127	4	17		8	
1469	149	5	8	1	3	7	49	1469
	5			1678			3	
	6			9	5		1	
		9	4	1678	2	5		

		3	5	678	4	1		
	7			2			5	
5	2			78			6	
		8	6	5	9	3		
	3		27	4	7		8	
469	49	5	8	1	3	7	49	469
	5			678			3	
	6			9	5		1	
		9	4	678	2	5		

In this book I call an easy sudoku puzzle 'gentle'. This indicates a level of complexity that can be tackled by beginners and casual sudoku solvers. However, no matter what level of puzzle you are attempting, there are a few strategies that will allow you to get to a solution more quickly.

The key strategy is to look for the lone number. In this example, all the options for box 5 have been pencilled in. At first there appear to be three places for the number 1 to go, but look between the 8 and 3 – there is a lone number 1. It was not otherwise obvious that the only square for the number 1 was row 6, column 5, as there is no number 1 in the immediate vicinity. Checking the adjacent boxes and relevant row and column would not provide an immediate answer either – but no other number can go in that box.

While our example uses pencil marks

to illustrate the rule, more experienced solvers are quite capable of doing this in their head.

Remember that this principal is true for boxes, rows and columns: if there is only one place for a number to go, then it is true for that box, and also the row and column it is in. You can eliminate all the other pencilled 1s in the box, row and column.

5	4			9			7	2
2	7	9			3	6		4
9		8	7		4			
1	9	4	8			7		
7				5		4		9
			4	7	9	2		1
4			6			3		
		2	9	3			4	7
3	1			4				6

Twins

Why limit yourself to one when sometimes two can do the job? In sudoku we can easily become blind to the obvious. You might look at a box and think there is no way of proving a number because it could go in more than one square, but there are times when the answer is staring you right in the face. Take the sudoku opposite. It's an example of a gentle puzzle. The solver has made a good start at finding the more obvious numbers, but having just solved the 9 in box 4 she's thinking about solving the 9 in box 1. It seems impossible, with just a 9 in row 1 and another in column 2 that immediately affect box 1.

5	4			9			7	2
2	7				3	6		4
9		8	7		4			
1	9	4	8			7		
7				5		4		9
			4	7	9	2		1
4		9	6			3		
		2	9	3			4	7
3	1	9		4				6

But look more carefully and you'll see that the 9 in row 8 precludes any 9 in row 8 of box 7. In addition, the 9 in column 2 eliminates the square to the right of the 4 in that box, leaving just the two squares above and below the 2 in box 7 available for the 9. **You've found a twin!**

Pencil in these 9s. While you don't know which of these two will end up as 9 in this box, what you do know is that the 9 has to be in column 3. Therefore a 9 cannot go in column 3 of box 1, leaving it the one available square in column 1.

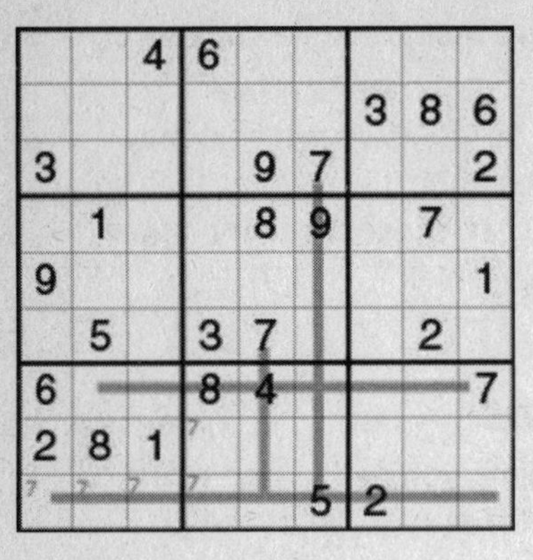

Triplets

In the previous example, our solver's twins did just as well as a solved number in helping to find her number. But if two unsolved squares can help you on your way, three *solved* numbers together certainly can.

Look at the sequence 2–8–1 in row 8. It can help you solve the 7 in box 8. The 7s in columns 5 and 6 place the 7s in box 8 at either 8,4 or 9,4. It is the 7 in row 7 that will provide sufficient clues to make a choice. Because there can be no more 7s in row 7, the 2–8–1 in row 8 forces the 7 in box 7 to be in row 9. Although you don't know which square it will be in, the unsolved trio will prove that no more 7s will go in row 9, putting our 7 in box 8 at row 8. A solved row or column of three squares in a box is good news. Try the same trick with the 3–8–6 in row 2 to see if this triplet helps to solve any more.

Eliminating the extraneous

We have looked at the basic number-finding strategies, but what if these are just not up to the job? Until now we have been casually pencilling in possible numbers, but there are many puzzles that will require you to be totally methodical in order to seek out and eliminate extraneous numbers.

If you have come to a point where obvious clues have dried up, before moving into unknown territory and beginning bifurcation (more on that later), you should ensure that you have actually found all the numbers you can. The first step towards achieving this is to pencil in *all* possible numbers in each square. It takes less time than you'd think to rattle off 'can 1 go', 'can 2 go', 'can 3 go', etc., while checking for these numbers in the square's box, row and column.

I've said it before in this introduction, but it doesn't hurt to repeat it: if something is true for one element then it has to be true for the other two associated elements. Let's flash back to something that we looked at earlier: twins. When we discovered this rule the grid wasn't so crowded as the section of sudoku on the left.

9	46	5
68	2	148
7	3	148
1	8	2
5	7	6
4	9	3
3	146	149
68	5	189
2	146	7

Now the twins are mixed with other numbers. It's not obvious, but the two 1s in the top box are twins. While we don't know which square is correct we do know that the 1 in that box will exclude any other 1s in column 3 right the way down to the bottom square. Using the twins eliminates two 1s in that column of the bottom box. Two 1s in one box helped eliminate 1s in another remote box.

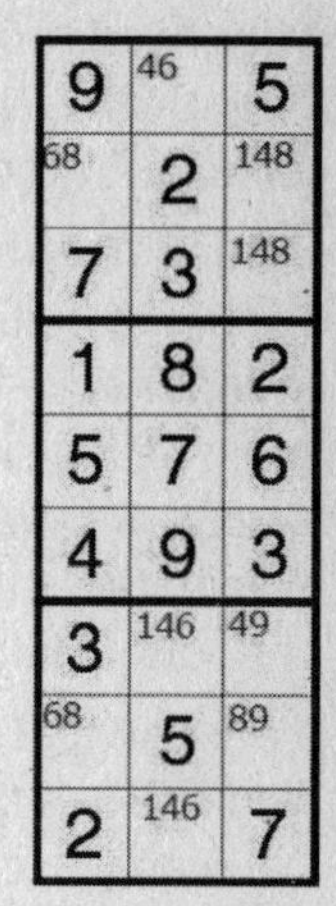

It is important to show you this, because while nothing is actually solved by this action, eliminating those 1s could make all the difference in proving a number. You'll be looking for things to help you move on in these kinds of crowded conditions. In a tough or diabolical puzzle it might allow you to proceed through to a solution without guessing.

Now you should **look for matching pairs** or trios of numbers in each column, row and box. You've seen matching pairs before: two squares in the same row, column or box that share a pair of numbers.

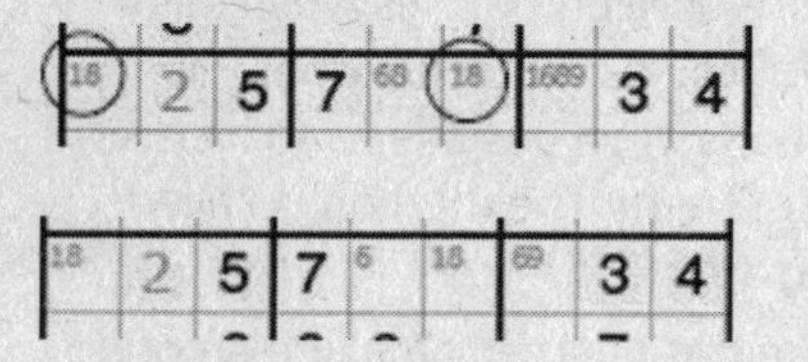

You can see what I mean in this illustration. In this row at column 1 there is a 1 8 and at column 6 there is also a 1 8. This matching pair is telling you that *only* either 1 or 8 is definitely at one or other of these locations. If that is true then **neither of these numbers can be at any other location in that row**. So you can eliminate the 1 and 8 in any other square of the row where they do not appear together. As you can see, this immediately solves the square at column 5. This rule can be applied to a row, column or box.

The number-sharing rule can be taken a stage further. Say you have three squares in a row that share the numbers 3, 7 and 9 and *only* those numbers. They may look like 3 7, 3 9, 7 9 or 3 7, 3 9, 3 7 9 or even 3 7 9, 3 7 9, 3 7 9. In the same way as our pairs example worked, you can eliminate all other occurrences of those numbers anywhere else on that row (or column or box). It will probably take a minute or so to get your head round this one, but like the pairs, where we were looking for two squares that held the same two numbers exclusively, here we are looking for three squares that contain three numbers exclusively.

Sometimes, the obvious simply needs to be stated, as in the case of two squares that contain 3 7 and 3 7 9. If the 3 and the 7 occur *only* in those two squares in a row, column or box, then either the 3 or 7 must be true in either one of the squares. So why is the 9 still in that square with what is so obviously a matching pair? Once that 9 has been eliminated, the pair matches and can now eliminate other 3s and 7s in the row, column or box. You could say this was a 'hidden' pair.

You may find such hidden pairs in rows, columns or boxes, but when you find one in a box, only when it has been converted to a true matching pair can you consider it as part of a row or column. Hidden trios work in exactly the same way, but are just more difficult to spot. Once you have assimilated the principle of two numbers sharing two squares exclusively or three numbers sharing three squares exclusively you will be well on the way to solving the most difficult sudoku.

Stepping up the sudoku action

In my previous *Daily Telegraph Sudoku* books I have gone to great lengths to explain how to solve the more difficult puzzles when all of the methods discussed thus far have failed. In a nutshell, what you have to do is to pick a likely pair of options in an unsolved square and attempt to solve the puzzle using one of them. The method is called bifurcation, which simply means taking a fork.

Since those books were published there has been an amazing amount of discussion on the internet about extending the more satisfying elimination methods to solve these sudoku. So much so that solvers have come up with schemes for most puzzles without resorting to guessing methods at all.

Let me emphasise at this juncture that the sudoku puzzles that may resist the methods discussed so far represent only a very small minority of the puzzles in this book. They will be among the diabolical and possibly some tough puzzles at the end. They are valid puzzles, and many advanced sudoku solvers have devised logic schemes (and computer programs) for solving them.

However, the wonderful thing about sudoku puzzles is that you don't have to be a genius or a computer programmer to solve even the most diabolical example. **If you are meticulous and patient and have mastered the gentle and moderate puzzles then you can solve every puzzle in this book.**

Hundreds (if not thousands) of *Daily Telegraph* readers, just ordinary, intelligent people, return correct solutions to the most difficult sudoku published in the newspaper's daily competition.

When all else fails

So how do they do it? I'll wager that when you bought this book you didn't think you'd be dealing with methodological analysis and bifurcation, but these are the technical terms for the process of picking a likely pair of numbers, choosing one and seeing where the number you have chosen gets you. Because you can be confident that *one* of the numbers will eventually produce a route to the solution, it is simply a matter of carefully analysing the options and testing your choice. If your first choice doesn't work out then you take the alternative route.

This final strategy is reserved for the most difficult of the diabolical and, occasionally, tough puzzles – when all else fails.

Think of a sudoku puzzle as a maze. Gentle and moderate puzzles have a simple path straight through to the exit. Tough and diabolical puzzles may have 'dead' ends which force you to try different routes. A tough puzzle is usually a more tortuous version of a moderate sudoku, but it may have one of these dead ends to cope with. Diabolical puzzles will have at least one, and maybe more paths that you could follow before finding the number that leads to a logical exit. The way to navigate this maze can be found in classical mythology, so allow me tell you a story.

Ariadne's thread

As well as creating sudoku puzzles, I also compile the giant general knowledge crossword for *The Daily Telegraph* weekend supplement, so excuse me if I put that hat on for a few moments to remind you briefly of the story of Ariadne's thread.

Ariadne was the daughter of King Minos of Crete, who conquered the Athenian nation. An unfortunate intimacy between Ariadne's mother and a bull resulted in the birth of the monster – half-bull, half-man – called the Minotaur, who was banished to spend his days in the

Labyrinth. King Minos, being something of a tyrant, called for tribute from Athens in the form of young men and women to be sacrificed to the Minotaur.

The young Athenian hero, Theseus, offered to accompany a group of the young unfortunates into the Labyrinth so that he could kill the Minotaur and save Athens from the cruel tribute. Ariadne fell in love with Theseus and, not wishing to see him lost in the Labyrinth once he had dealt with her bovine half-brother, she provided him with a means of escape – a silken thread. Theseus had simply to unwind it while he went through the Labyrinth; should he come to a dead end he could rewind it to the point where he had made a choice of paths and continue his search using the alternative route. The scheme worked out beautifully, the Minotaur was slain, Theseus found his way back out of the Labyrinth and Ariadne . . . well, she got her ball of string back, no doubt.

Replacing my sudoku hat, I hope that this tale of Ariadne's thread has served to illustrate this method of solving tough and diabolical sudoku.

Solving a diabolical puzzle

In its structure there is no difference between a tough sudoku and a diabolical puzzle. The grading is only increased because in a diabolical puzzle there are more places where clues can run out and more apparent dead ends.

	8	4	5	69	1		7	2
			4		8	1		5
1	5			3	2	4	9	8
		9	8			5		1
8		1		5				9
4	6	5	9	1	3	2	8	7
7	4	3	1	8	5	9	2	6
5	9			4	6		1	3
	1		3		9		5	4

Take this example. For clarity's sake we'll ignore all the 'pencil' marks on the grid except for the first pair: at 1,5 we have either a 6 or a 9. There is at least one other pair our solver could have chosen on the grid, but this was the first, so let's be logical and use that. Our solver chooses to try the 6 first, and the following diagram shows the numbers she is able to complete using this number in bold grey.

9	8	4	5	[69] 6	1	3	7	2
2	3	7	4	9	8	1	6	5
1	5	6	7	3	2	4	9	8
3	7	9	8	2	4	5		1
8	2	1		5	7	6	3	9
4	6	5	9	1	3	2	8	7
7	4	3	1	8	5	9	2	6
5	9	8	2	4	6	7	1	3
6	1	2	3	7	9	8	5	4

	8	4	5	[69] 9	1		7	2
9			4		8	1		5
1	5			3	2	4	9	8
		9	8			5		1
8		1		5				9
4	6	5	9	1	3	2	8	7
7	4	3	1	8	5	9	2	6
5	9			4	6		1	3
	1		3		9		5	4

6	8	4	5	9	1	[36] 3	7	2
9	3	2	4	7	8	1	6	5
1	5	7	6	3	2	4	9	8
3	2	9	8	6	7	5	4	1
8	7	1	2	5	4	6	3	9
4	6	5	9	1	3	2	8	7
7	4	3	1	8	5	9	2	6
5	9	8	7	4	6		1	3
	1	6	3	2	9	7	5	4

But with just two squares to fill, look at what we have: at 4,8 the box needs a 4 to complete it, but there is already a 4 in that row at 4,6. Similarly, at 5,4 that box needs a 6, but one already exists in that row at 5,7. No second guess was needed to prove that at 1,5 the 6 was incorrect.

So our solver returns to 1,5 and tries the 9. Now we are able to prove the 9 at 2,1, but nothing else is obvious; every square is left with options. In this case we could leave both 9s, because we proved without doubt that the 6 at 1,5 could not be correct, but if the 6 had simply left us without sufficient clues, as the 9 did, we wouldn't know which was true. Rather than start a new, uncertain path it is better to return to the situation we were in before we chose at 1,5 and find another square to try from. This is a base we know to be true.

In this illustration we can see that our solver looks at square 1,7 where the choice is between a 3 and a 6. Choosing the 3 she finds herself on a path that takes her to just two more to go but discovers that a 2 is required to complete box 7. There's already a 2 in that row at 9,5. In box 9 she needs an 8, but there's an 8 in row 8 already. She now winds in the thread to get back to 1,7 where 3 was chosen last time. Trying 6 here will lead to a solution.

The last word

Every day I receive a few emails from *Daily Telegraph* solvers who tell me how they struggled on Tuesday's moderate puzzle, but flew through the diabolical example on Friday. My answer is always that my grading of puzzles is subjective. I have no way of knowing what mistakes a solver might make, how experienced he or she is or whether he or she is suffering from a bad day or not. The same puzzle may take one person thirty minutes and another two hours, and it's not always down to the level of experience of the solver. Also, some people have an innate ability to spot the clues. With practice, others develop this ability without realising it.

No matter how good or bad you are at sudoku, what I can guarantee is that these puzzles will give you a good mental workout. As keep fit for the brain, in my experience as a puzzle setter, sudoku is as good as it gets. Have fun.

Acknowlegements

Since the first *Daily Telegraph Sudoku* book was published in May many new solvers have contacted me through the website dedicated to *Daily Telegraph* and *Sunday Telegraph* sudoku at www.sudoku.org.uk, and I'd like to thank them for sharing their helpful solving suggestions and tips, many of which may be found in the website forum.

I must also thank the thousands of *Daily Telegraph* readers who have contacted me since the puzzle first appeared in their newspaper. Their suggestions and unbounded enthusiasm for sudoku is reflected in the size of my daily postbag. Many of their comments, questions and suggestions have helped to shape this tutorial.

My thanks also to Telegraph Books Publishing Director Morven Knowles and Kate Harvey of Pan Macmillan. Between them they have managed to keep me on schedule to produce this third volume of *Sudoku* in as many months, despite my trait for leaving everything to the very last second.

Michael Mepham

Frome, Somerset, 2005

Extreme sudoku

If you thought that diabolical sudoku was the ultimate sudoku challenge, here's something to make you think again: a three-dimensional sudoku cube.

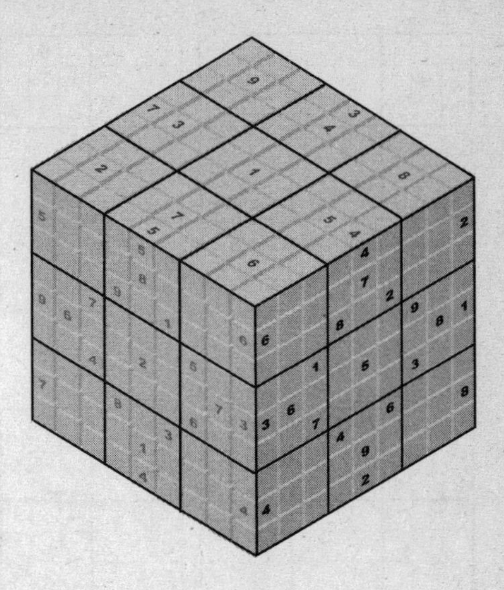

In the puzzle shown on the next page you will see nine sudoku 'boards'. These represent slices of the cube illustrated here from the top layer downwards. However, they could just as easily have been slices from the front or side – each 'slice' will work out as a valid sudoku solution.

All you have to remember is that any number you place has to follow the sudoku rules, not only in the plane that you are working on, but also in the vertical plane that passes through it. You can get the idea from this illustration. The hidden 6 right at the centre (it's on Layer 5 overleaf) is the only 6 for that row, column and vertical column and also for the associated 3 x 3 boxes.

Don't attempt to work it out on the page. Copy the worksheet printed at the end of this book and then carefully transcribe the clue numbers.

The solution is at the end of the book.

				3				
	9			4			8	
7	3			1			5	4
	2			7			6	
				5				

Layer 1

3				9				2
				7				
		9	2		4	7		
		4	7		8	6		
1	9						8	7
		3	9		1	4		
		1	4		5	8		
				1				
5				8				6

Layer 2

			4		5			
	3		6		9		5	
3	8						4	2
				7				
6	1						3	8
	9		5		2		8	
			9		1			

Layer 3

		6				3		
2		4				6		9
4		5				9		1
		7				5		

Layer 4

4	2			7			6	1
6	1						3	8
				9				
8		3		6		4		5
				1				
5	4						9	6
9	6			2			7	3

Layer 5

		8				2		
9		1				8		3
1		6				3		7
		4				6		

Layer 6

			9		1			
	5		7		8		1	
5	4						9	6
				2				
7	3						5	4
	8		1		6		4	
			8		3			

Layer 7

6				5				8
				9				
		5	8		3	9		
		3	9		1	4		
2	5						1	9
		6	5		2	3		
		2	3		7	1		
				2				
7				1				4

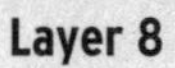

Layer 8

				8				
	6			2			7	
3	8			9			4	2
	5			3			1	
				4				

Layer 9

The Puzzles

9			8		2			6
			9		3			
3		7				4		8
		2	5		7	8		
	4						3	
		6	1		4	2		
2		8				1		3
			3		9			
6			4		8			2

		1					4	
		9				8		3
		7	5	8	3			
	5	2		4				
	3		1		2		8	
				7		1	2	
			7	2	1	9		
2		4				3		
	1					7		

7		1	5		3	4		8
		9				5		
	5	8				1	3	
			7	5	2			
				1				
			6	3	4			
	1	6				7	9	
		7				6		
5		4	8		6	3		1

6	9						8	3
	1		2		6		4	
		8				7		
		9		5		4		
7								9
		3		9		5		
		2				3		
	3		5		9		7	
8	4						9	6

8				6	5		1	4
					7	5		
3					2		8	
		7			1	3		
1								8
		2	9			6		
	2		6					5
		8	1					
6	3		2	7				9

5	6						2	8
	2	8		6		4	3	
1	3						5	6
			9		7			
				8				
			4		2			
6	4						8	5
	8	1		5		2	9	
2	9						7	1

			9		3		4	7
	2			5				
1	3		6					
				8	2			1
6	8						7	3
5			3	1				
					7		5	8
				6			1	
7	4		5		1			

6	2		8					
	1	5					4	
7				9		3		
		4				9		6
8			2		4			5
2		1				4		
		6		3				4
	7					6	9	
					2		5	3

	3				1		9	
2		8			7			
1						2		7
	5	3		8	9	7	2	
				6				
	7	6	3	4		1	5	
7		9						8
			9			4		2
	4		5				3	

SUDOKU 3 GENTLE

			3	8				1
6								4
		9	4		5		2	6
				4				
	1		2		8		9	
				1				
7	5		1		3	6		
9								8
4				6	2			

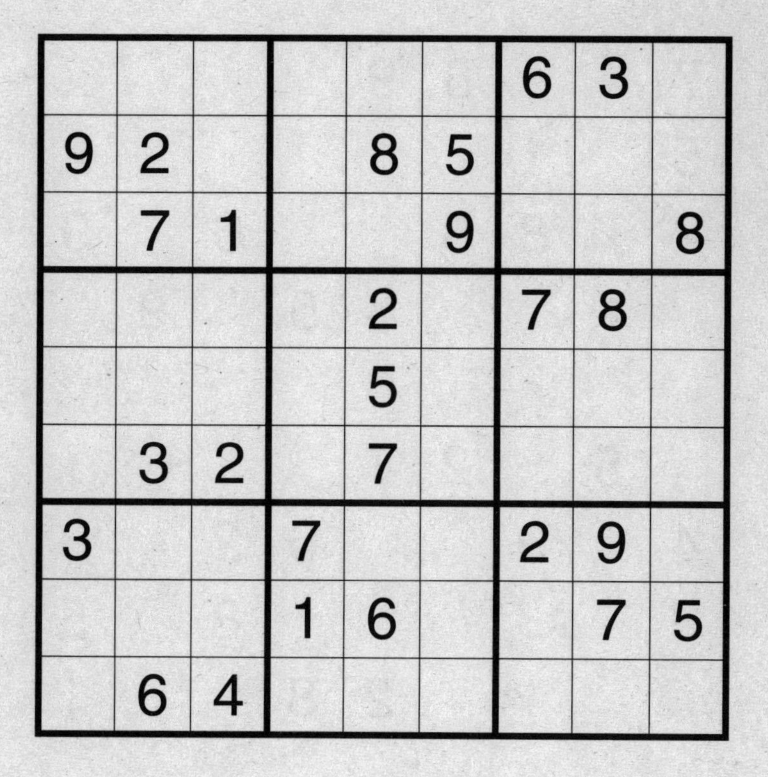

						6	3	
9	2			8	5			
	7	1			9			8
				2		7	8	
				5				
	3	2		7				
3			7			2	9	
			1	6			7	5
	6	4						

7			8	9				
5		1						2
2		8	5			6		9
				8	5		9	
				6				
	5		2	7				
4		9			6	2		3
3						8		5
				2	8			1

8			3		1			4
			9		4			
	6	9				2	3	
		8	6		3	5		
	3						6	
		4	7		9	3		
	7	1				9	8	
			1		5			
3			2		7			5

	3	5	1				8	
			3			9		
					6		7	
		9	7		3			8
4	5						2	3
3			4		2	6		
	6		8					
		1			7			
	4				9	7	1	

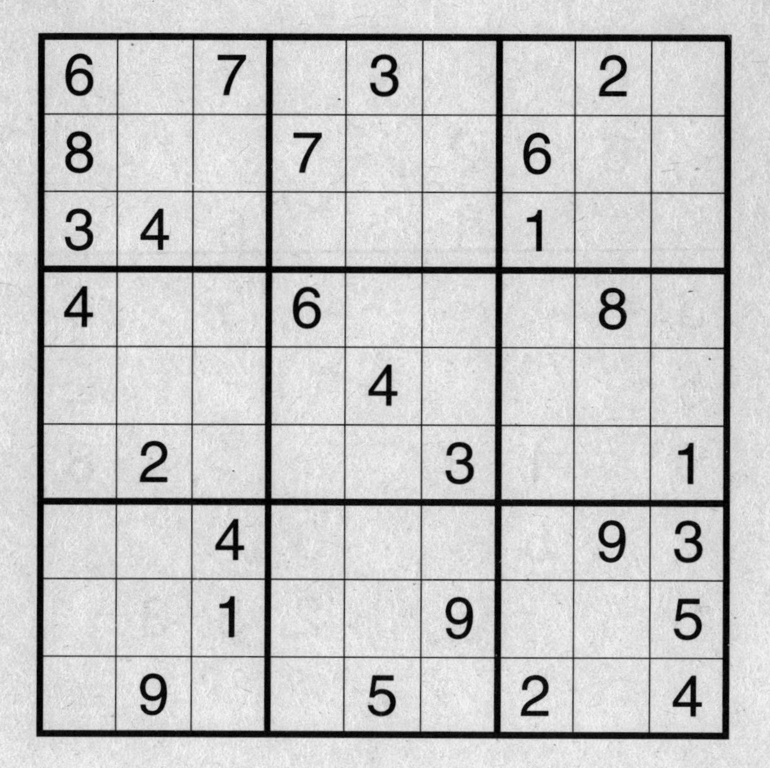

6		7		3			2	
8			7			6		
3	4					1		
4			6				8	
				4				
	2				3			1
		4					9	3
		1			9			5
	9			5		2		4

	8			9				
	6	4	2					1
			1			6		
3	4					5		6
5								2
9		1					4	8
		5			3			
6					2	8	3	
				7			1	

4			6		7			2
	5		3		9		8	
8		6				9		3
			8		1			
3								4
			9		5			
5		4				2		7
	3		5		2		4	
2			4		3			1

1	2					8		
		3	5				1	
		6		2		9		
		8		1			9	
	5		3		2		8	
	7			4		3		
		4		5		7		
	1				7	6		
		9					3	5

9						7		6
3				6	2			
				3		8		
	4	5			7	1		2
	3						6	
2		9	8			3	4	
		4		2				
			4	5				8
8		1						4

3	8						7	4
		5	4		2	9		
7								2
		7	6	9	1	4		
		9	7	8	4	3		
9								6
		8	5		3	7		
6	7						8	3

6							4	
	5		6	7				3
	2					7		6
	7		3			4		
	9		7		6		8	
		3			4		6	
2		5					3	
3				1	8		7	
	6							5

2	9				1			3
		4	5		8	2		
	1		2			9		
7	4							
			6		2			
							6	5
		9			3		2	
		7	8		5	1		
8			9				7	4

			5	2	8	3		6
5							1	9
6		2		3		8		
		7	4		2	5		
		5		6		1		4
7	6							5
1		4	6	8	3			

	2			9		1		6
							4	
4				2	1		8	
			9	1		8	5	
			3		8			
	8	1		5	4			
	5		2	6				1
	9							
1		6		3			9	

1		9				7		6
		2	4		1	5		
4	7						2	3
			6		7			
2								7
			1		9			
3	9						1	2
		1	9		3	4		
7		4				3		8

			3		9			
	8	3	5					7
		4			8	9		5
				8	7			6
	4						8	
1			6	5				
6		1	2			4		
4					5	3	2	
			7		4			

	5			1	4		6	
8		4						9
	1		2					
6	7							3
		8	7		9	1		
1							8	2
					8		2	
3						4		5
	2		4	5			9	

		8	3	5	1		6	
						7		
6			2					
2		6	1				7	
1	9						8	5
	5				9	2		4
					2			8
		4						
	1		5	3	8	4		

	5	2				9	7	
		6		8		5		
8	7						1	6
		1	2		6	3		
		5	9		4	6		
5	4						2	9
		7		5		8		
	6	3				1	4	

					6	4		
5			9					
	2				5		9	7
6		8	4		1			3
		4				2		
1			5		8	6		4
4	3		8				6	
					4			2
		9	7					

		1	6		3	9		
	7		9		5		4	
4								1
		9	3		7	2		
2								4
		7	4		1	8		
7								9
	1		7		2		5	
		5	1		4	3		

1							5	
		6	3	8	2	9		
	4		1			2		
					7		9	
		4				5		
	5		9					
		1			3		7	
		3	6	9	1	8		
	8							9

			6			2		8
	6			9	1			
	7						9	1
5			1		2			
	3	9	7		6	8	2	
			3		9			4
6	9						8	
			5	6			3	
2		7			8			

		9	5				6	4
		3						
		8			9	1	5	
	1			6	5			7
			8		4			
6			7	3			9	
	3	7	1			2		
						7		
8	4				6	5		

3	6			1				
5			3				4	7
	7	4					6	
	3	6		4	2			
			8		3			
			6	5		4	3	
	2					8	5	
7	5				8			4
				6			9	2

	8			5				
1			9	7				
5		9		6		7		
6		4	8				1	
8	7						2	9
	9				6	8		4
		5		8		9		2
				4	3			1
				2			3	

5			3		9			8
		8	5	2	4	6		
9								4
		1				2		
2	4						3	5
		3				8		
4								3
		9	6	5	3	4		
1			4		7			9

					2		5	
3						4		
5	2			4		6		1
			2	9	3		8	
		1				9		
	9		7	8	1			
2		8		7			1	3
		5						8
	6		8					

		8				7		
	9	3	7	1			5	
6				2			1	
1	2		6					
8								9
					4		6	1
	6			8				4
	8			5	2	9	7	
		7				8		

		1		8				
5	3		2			8	4	9
							1	
		2			1	9		6
1								5
6		3	5			2		
	8							
3	1	6			5		9	4
				9		6		

	1	6	7		8	2	5	
		4				8		
7	9						6	3
			8		6			
	8						4	
			2		7			
4	3						8	1
		7				6		
	6	1	9		5	4	7	

		3	2		4	8		
	9		1		6		2	
5								6
			5		1			
8	3						1	5
			3		7			
6								9
	2		7		8		3	
		5	9		2	6		

	7			8				
6			5		4			8
			6				5	7
		8			9	7		
	5	4				9	1	
		3	4			2		
5	3				8			
9			1		6			4
				2			9	

	1	9	7					
2				9				5
			3		4	8		
4							9	6
			2		8			
5	3							2
		6	4		7			
9				5				1
					3	4	5	

		3						2
4	8			5	1			7
			8		6			
		4			9	7		5
	3						9	
5		6	1			4		
			5		7			
7			2	1			5	4
2						3		

	3						9	
		8		2		4		
	4		7		6			3
3			2	7				4
	6						7	
7				5	8			9
8			3		5		4	
		6		4		2		
	7						1	

				9	6		1	
		3	5		7			2
	1		4		8			5
4	9					5		
		1					2	7
7			1		5		8	
3			7		4	6		
	6		9	2				

9	7				5	4		
				8	3	6		
	3			7				
		8					5	6
5		4				7		9
3	2					1		
				5			7	
		2	9	4				
		9	8				4	2

			8	5				3
			2	4		8	6	1
					1			
6	3			8			7	
		7				3		
	4			1			5	6
			1					
7	6	8		3	9			
4				6	5			

	5	9						7
						2		6
		7		3	1			
9				6	7		8	
	4						6	
	1		3	8				5
			7	5		6		
2		1						
3						4	9	

						9		
	8	2			1		5	
7			9	2				
				5	4			3
2		9	1		7	8		4
8			2	6				
				1	6			8
	2		5			4	1	
		4						

3		6		5				4
	5		1		3	2	9	6
		1	7					
	8	5				1	6	
					2	3		
7	1	9	2		4		5	
5				7		9		2

8	5		4		1		7	3
6		2				5		4
		7	3	5	8	4		
		8	6	1	4	2		
9		6				8		2
2	3		8		6		9	5

					7	4		
		6			8		7	
4				6		8	3	
	2		7					6
9	8						1	7
6					3		5	
	4	5		3				8
	3		4			7		
		1	8					

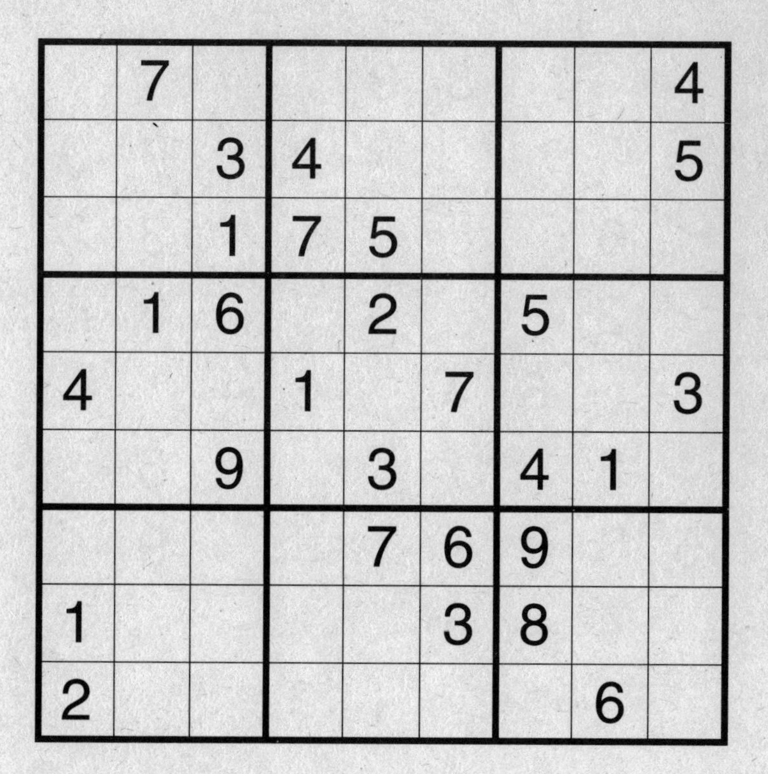

	7							4
		3	4					5
		1	7	5				
	1	6		2		5		
4			1		7			3
		9		3		4	1	
				7	6	9		
1					3	8		
2							6	

			8	3				
3					2		7	
	6						3	2
	2				7		8	4
		6	4		5	1		
4	8		1				6	
5	3						9	
	4		6					7
				1	3			

		1	8		3			
6							2	3
		4	9				5	6
		6		2			1	
	8						7	
	7			8		6		
7	6				1	5		
3	2							1
			6		9	7		

		7			8	2	9	
				1			7	6
	9				6			
3	5					8		7
			8		3			
9		8					4	3
			1				5	
5	4			6				
	8	2	4			9		

								9
						7		6
8		3	1				5	2
2					1			5
	3		2		6		1	
1			5					7
9	1				7	2		4
4		2						
3								

						3	7	5
				9			6	
8				7	2			
	4				7		1	9
		2	9		3	6		
9	5		8				2	
			2	8				6
	3			5				
7	2	1						

			1					9
		2	7	5		6	1	
8				9	3			2
		9	2				7	
				1				
	2				5	1		
7			8	2				6
	8	6		4	7	9		
1					6			

	9	6	5					
4		3	7		8			
2				3				1
	4				5			
7	6						2	5
			6				8	
1				8				6
			3		7	1		4
					1	9	3	

	5		2		3		1	
	4	1				9	6	
		2	1		9	6		
7	3						9	8
		9	4		8	3		
	9	5				8	4	
	6		9		2		3	

	4	9				8	2	
			3		9			
6								4
		6	4		1	3		
	8						7	
		3	5		2	1		
5								6
			1		8			
	9	4				7	8	

7	5						3	2
	9		3		1		7	
6	3						1	4
			4		9			
8								3
			5		6			
1	2						4	9
	8		1		3		2	
9	7						8	6

		7			9		5	
9	2			3				7
	1			8				
2		1	3					9
	6						4	
5					6	7		1
				5			2	
7				1			6	3
	9		6			4		

		8					1	9
			9	5	7	6		
		6		3				
		5		9			2	
3		9				1		5
	6			1		8		
				2		9		
		2	8	7	6			
8	7					5		

			9	1				3
2				5				
6					8	9		
3		7	8	6			5	
		5				2		
	1			9	5	4		6
		6	2					7
				4				2
5				8	6			

		4			1		5	6
9	2		6			1		
								4
			7			4		8
	4		1		3		2	
2		5			8			
8								
		3			2		6	1
6	1		4			3		

	1		9			5	7	
				7	6			
					2	1		6
1		5	4					
9	2						1	4
					1	3		9
4		8	5					
			2	3				
	3	7			9		4	

					6			
			7	8		3		9
			5	1			8	
9		2			8	6		
	7	1				8	3	
		8	4			1		2
	4			2	7			
2		9		5	4			
			8					

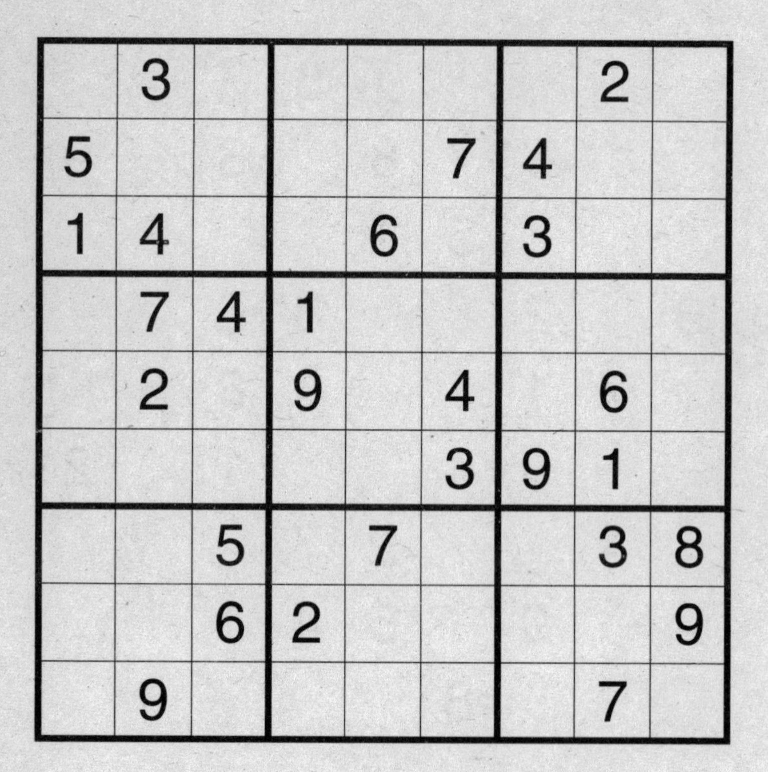

	3						2	
5					7	4		
1	4			6		3		
	7	4	1					
	2		9		4		6	
					3	9	1	
		5		7			3	8
		6	2					9
	9						7	

	2	3			9	8		
		7					2	9
			4			5		
			9		3			2
		1	6		2	9		
2			7		4			
		2			6			
4	6					1		
		9	3			2	8	

		9			3			7
	8		4			5		
4			5					
9	3		6			7		
2			1		7			6
		5			9		1	2
					2			8
		4			1		7	
1			3			6		

			5	6		8	9	
	8			3		5		7
			1					
		1			6		2	3
		9				7		
8	6		7			4		
					1			
6		7		4			3	
	9	4		5	3			

5				2			1	9
	1	9				2		
		6			1		4	5
1					4		7	
				3				
	5		1					2
8	2		6			4		
		3				6	5	
9	6			1				7

						1	5	
	8	5	6	1				3
		6		2				
		8		3				
3	5		4		9		1	2
				5		7		
				9		2		
8				6	5	9	7	
	1	9						

	5		1		7		4	
	2		5		3		7	
1								2
		8	6		1	3		
2								6
		3	4		2	1		
9								5
	8		7		4		1	
	4		3		9		8	

7		3				8		9
			8		2			
8	9						2	1
		7	9		4	6		
	5						9	
		9	2		3	7		
2	6						5	3
			1		6			
4		8				9		6

2						7	5	
					3			1
		8			6	9		
		7	8	2				3
		9	3		7	1		
3				1	9	8		
		6	9			3		
8			7					
	4	3						5

						3		4
		2		5				
	1	6	4			9	2	
				9	5	4		
5		7				1		6
		9	8	6				
	3	1			7	8	4	
				1		7		
8		5						

		2	5		3		8	
					4	5	1	9
	5	9	8					
							4	1
4								5
8	2							
					2	6	9	
2	3	6	9					
	9		3		8	2		

7					8			
9						4	3	1
			4	1			9	7
		1				7		
2			7		6			8
		8				5		
6	2			7	3			
1	4	3						6
			1					3

1		7	3	2				6
					1	7		
		5	7					9
	1			7				
	7		9		6		1	
				4			8	
8					4	3		
		2	5					
6				8	7	4		5

4		7			8		2	
9						4	7	6
1								
			1	6				7
		9	2		3	1		
2				8	7			
								4
7	1	8						5
	6		7			3		2

	2					1		
	8		2				3	6
4				9		8		
2					1			
	7		9		8		5	
			5					1
		4		7				5
3	5				6		8	
		9					4	

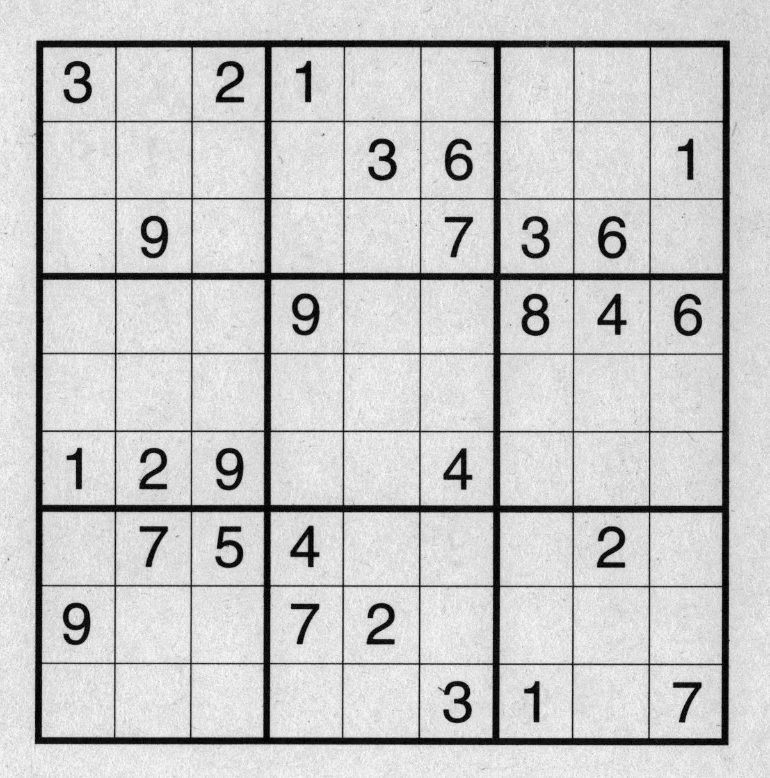

3		2	1					
				3	6			1
	9				7	3	6	
			9			8	4	6
1	2	9			4			
	7	5	4				2	
9			7	2				
					3	1		7

					4	1	7	
9				3			4	8
		8			6			
1	6				7		8	
5								1
	8		1				6	3
			3			8		
2	3			5				6
	1	9	4					

				2	8			4
	9	1	6		7		8	
		3		9				
			5		4	8	7	
				6				
	1	4	8		9			
				8		6		
	5		1		6	9	3	
7			9	3				

7			2		4			6
	2	6				5	8	
		7	9	2	5	3		
6								7
		9	4	6	7	8		
	5	4				6	1	
2			6		9			8

	8		9				3	
5			4					
		6			5			8
		8		9		6	1	
6	1						7	5
	5	3		7		2		
7			6			3		
					2			7
	3				1		9	

3		5	2				9	
			9	4				
9		2						
1			8		9	5		4
	9						8	
2		8	6		4			3
						3		6
				9	1			
	1				3	2		9

8		7				3		2
	2			4			7	
6	5						8	9
			4		2			
	7						6	
			3		1			
7	6						9	5
	1			9			2	
5		9				1		7

			1			8		9
	8		4				3	6
1	6		8					2
							5	
		7	9		4	6		
	2							
9					7		6	1
4	1				8		2	
2		6			5			

		2	6			3		7
6							9	
		4	2		9	1		
				3	7	6	1	
				4				
	5	3	1	9				
		5	7		8	9		
	7							1
4		9			1	5		

	8		5	6			3	
		7		1		2		
2					7	1		9
			2			5		
	2						9	
		4			6			
4		6	7					3
		1		5		8		
	9			4	3		7	

				8			7	
		6			4	1		8
5	8				1	2		
							6	4
	6		7		3		1	
9	5							
		5	1				4	9
6		2	9			8		
	7			3				

	2							5
			4		1	8		3
	3		8			9		
	9	2			4			
1		3				4		7
			9			5	6	
		6			7		4	
2		8	1		6			
3							5	

	1	5		2			3	
				3				
	3	8	9					
	7	9				8	4	6
8								3
6	2	3				1	7	
					8	7	1	
				7				
	4			9		5	2	

		4	2			8		9
7							2	
3			6			7		
				1	9	6		
8	1						9	4
		9	5	4				
		6			1			7
	2							1
5		1			3	2		

	5				7	8		3
			4					
1	6					4	7	
6			8	1				
5	2						6	8
				7	5			2
	8	5					4	6
					1			
3		4	5				9	

	3						8	
	4			8	2			6
				6		4	7	5
	2		6			1		
1								7
		8			5		3	
3	8	1		9				
7			5	3			2	
	5						1	

7		5	2		6	9		3
	9						5	
		3				7		
		7	4		3	2		
	4						3	
		1	9		5	4		
		8				5		
	7						2	
3		2	5		7	8		4

				7	6		9	
				4	8			
	2	4				8	7	
		2				6	3	5
		6				7		
1	7	3				4		
	5	7				1	4	
			9	5				
	4		7	3				

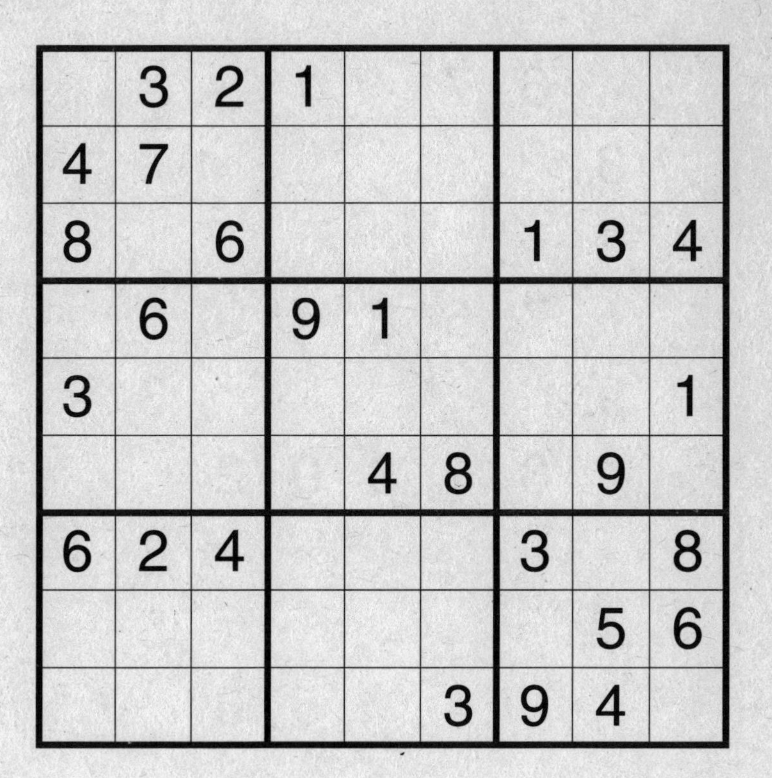

	3	2	1					
4	7							
8		6				1	3	4
	6		9	1				
3								1
				4	8		9	
6	2	4				3		8
							5	6
					3	9	4	

		6	7		1	3		
	3						7	
1								8
		7	6	8	4	9		
	9						3	
		8	1	3	9	2		
6								1
	4						5	
		9	4		5	6		

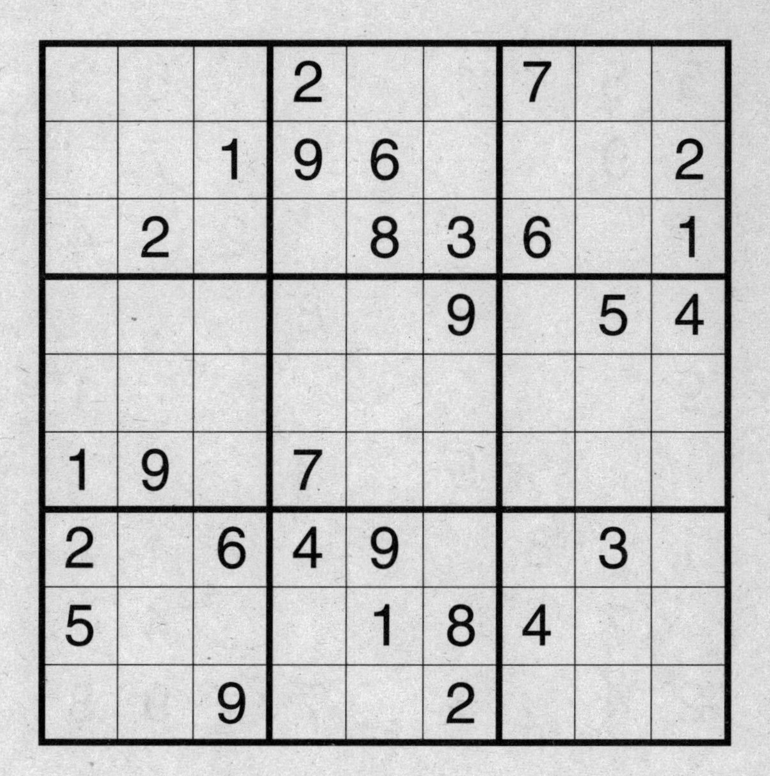

			2			7		
		1	9	6				2
	2			8	3	6		1
					9		5	4
1	9		7					
2		6	4	9			3	
5				1	8	4		
		9			2			

5	8		1		4		6	9
	9						7	
7		3				2		4
			5		8			
9								1
			9		3			
1		8				7		2
	7						4	
2	4		3		7		9	8

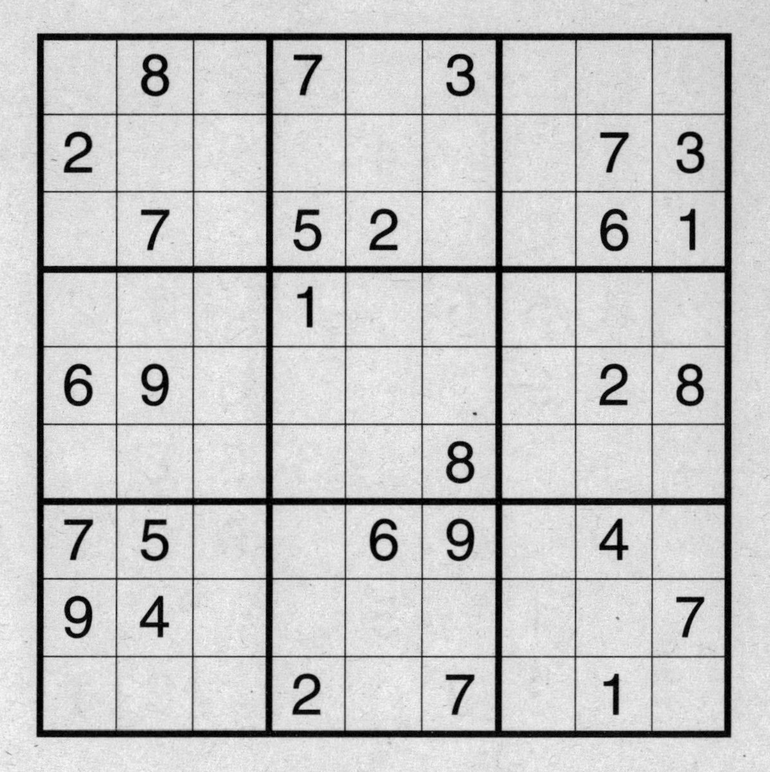

	8		7		3			
2							7	3
	7		5	2			6	1
			1					
6	9						2	8
					8			
7	5			6	9		4	
9	4							7
			2		7		1	

9					1	2		
				4		9		
	4	2		8				
	3	5	6					2
	7	9				3	4	
4					3	5	8	
				3		6	5	
		1		5				
		3	9					1

8	3			6				5
	5					2	4	
		4						8
3					9	1		
	4		1		6		8	
		2	8					4
9						8		
	6	3					9	
4				7			5	3

4				8			5	
		3			5			2
				2	3	7		1
7	4			9				
1								6
				5			1	4
8		1	3	6				
9			8			5		
	7			4				8

		3						
	5	7			3			9
			4	7	2		3	
1		6	5				7	
		4				5		
	9				4	8		1
	3		1	4	8			
5			9			1	4	
						2		

5			9		7			3
	7			3			8	
3	6						1	9
		3	2		9	1		
		5	3		1	9		
8	3						4	1
	9			4			5	
6			8		2			7

		7	4					
		3		2	6			8
4				7	3			9
				1			8	
2			7		9			4
	7			3				
6			5	9				2
3			8	4		7		
					2	1		

	1		2			5		4
6	3	9		5		7		
					9			
7	4		3					
		2				3		
					7		2	1
			1					
		6		3		2	4	8
4		3			8		7	

7	3			2				4
						7		5
	4			6				
		4			1			9
	8		6		5		3	
5			9			8		
				1			5	
6		1						
8				7			1	3

2					6	8		
6								9
		9			8	7		
8		5		3	2			1
			5		7			
7			8	1		9		3
		3	2			6		
9								8
		8	1					7

	8	1			7			
	9		5					
4	3	5			2			
5	2					8	9	
		9				2		
	6	7					3	4
			6			3	8	1
					5		2	
			3			4	6	

		1				9		
	8		7	4	9		1	
4								3
		2	3		7	1		
1								2
		7	2		4	5		
3								9
	5		1	3	2		7	
		8				3		

2			5		9			1
	5		2		8		3	
		3				7		
		2				4		
1	8						7	3
		9				5		
		8				3		
	2		6		7		9	
9			3		5			6

			6		8			1
7			9	3		6	2	
	4							
		9		1			5	
5		3				4		7
	2			5		9		
							6	
	9	1		6	5			3
2			1		3			

	2		6		5		7	
	8			4			3	
9								1
		4	1		7	5		
8								4
		2	4		8	9		
7								6
	4			8			9	
	5		7		1		8	

			1		3	9		5
9					4			
	5		2	6			8	
		2					7	
6			3		7			8
	4					2		
	8			5	2		1	
			6					9
3		6	7		1			

7				5				
8		4	3			6	5	
6				4			1	
			1	3	6			
		5				3		
			7	2	5			
	3			6				2
	4	6			2	9		3
				1				6

	8				7		6	
2				1				
1		4				2		7
4					2		5	
	2	1				6	8	
	7		3					2
7		6				4		8
				3				9
	1		8				7	

			9	2				
		6	8		3			
1	9			7				6
2	3			4		1		
		1				7		
		8		3			2	9
7				8			9	1
			5		7	2		
				6	4			

	9							2
	5	2		9			7	
	3	7			5	4		
					8			6
	1	8				2	4	
7			4					
		4	9			7	3	
	8			4		5	9	
1							2	

1	8			4				
	9		2			1		7
			1		9			3
				2		8		
3	7						2	9
		4		7				
2			3		1			
6		7			2		3	
				6			5	1

				6		1		
	8			5		9		4
			8		4	6	3	
					2		4	
5		3				7		6
	7		5					
	9	7	2		5			
6		2		4			9	
		4		9				

			3		6			5
	9		4					6
				8	2	1		
	2					4	6	
	6		9		4		7	
	5	8					3	
		9	8	4				
5					9		1	
8			1		7			

8			2		9			7
		9	3		6	2		
3								6
		7	6		1	3		
	3						5	
		8	9		3	6		
1								8
		3	1		8	7		
9			4		7			3

The Solutions

1

9	5	4	8	7	2	3	1	6
8	6	1	9	4	3	7	2	5
3	2	7	6	5	1	4	9	8
1	3	2	5	9	7	8	6	4
7	4	9	2	8	6	5	3	1
5	8	6	1	3	4	2	7	9
2	9	8	7	6	5	1	4	3
4	1	5	3	2	9	6	8	7
6	7	3	4	1	8	9	5	2

2

3	8	1	2	9	7	5	4	6
5	2	9	6	1	4	8	7	3
6	4	7	5	8	3	2	9	1
1	5	2	8	4	9	6	3	7
7	3	6	1	5	2	4	8	9
4	9	8	3	7	6	1	2	5
8	6	3	7	2	1	9	5	4
2	7	4	9	6	5	3	1	8
9	1	5	4	3	8	7	6	2

3

7	2	1	5	9	3	4	6	8
3	6	9	4	8	1	5	7	2
4	5	8	2	6	7	1	3	9
9	4	3	7	5	2	8	1	6
6	7	5	9	1	8	2	4	3
1	8	2	6	3	4	9	5	7
8	1	6	3	2	5	7	9	4
2	3	7	1	4	9	6	8	5
5	9	4	8	7	6	3	2	1

4

6	9	4	7	1	5	2	8	3
3	1	7	2	8	6	9	4	5
5	2	8	9	3	4	7	6	1
2	8	9	6	5	3	4	1	7
7	5	1	4	2	8	6	3	9
4	6	3	1	9	7	5	2	8
9	7	2	8	6	1	3	5	4
1	3	6	5	4	9	8	7	2
8	4	5	3	7	2	1	9	6

5

8	7	9	3	6	5	2	1	4
2	1	4	8	9	7	5	6	3
3	5	6	4	1	2	9	8	7
4	6	7	5	8	1	3	9	2
1	9	3	7	2	6	4	5	8
5	8	2	9	3	4	6	7	1
7	2	1	6	4	9	8	3	5
9	4	8	1	5	3	7	2	6
6	3	5	2	7	8	1	4	9

6

5	6	9	3	7	4	1	2	8
7	2	8	5	6	1	4	3	9
1	3	4	2	9	8	7	5	6
8	1	6	9	3	7	5	4	2
4	7	2	6	8	5	9	1	3
9	5	3	4	1	2	8	6	7
6	4	7	1	2	9	3	8	5
3	8	1	7	5	6	2	9	4
2	9	5	8	4	3	6	7	1

7

8	6	5	9	2	3	1	4	7
4	2	7	1	5	8	9	3	6
1	3	9	6	7	4	8	2	5
3	9	4	7	8	2	5	6	1
6	8	1	4	9	5	2	7	3
5	7	2	3	1	6	4	8	9
9	1	6	2	4	7	3	5	8
2	5	3	8	6	9	7	1	4
7	4	8	5	3	1	6	9	2

8

6	2	3	8	4	7	5	1	9
9	1	5	3	2	6	8	4	7
7	4	8	5	9	1	3	6	2
5	3	4	1	7	8	9	2	6
8	9	7	2	6	4	1	3	5
2	6	1	9	5	3	4	7	8
1	5	6	7	3	9	2	8	4
3	7	2	4	8	5	6	9	1
4	8	9	6	1	2	7	5	3

9

5	3	7	8	2	1	6	9	4
2	6	8	4	9	7	3	1	5
1	9	4	6	5	3	2	8	7
4	5	3	1	8	9	7	2	6
9	2	1	7	6	5	8	4	3
8	7	6	3	4	2	1	5	9
7	1	9	2	3	4	5	6	8
3	8	5	9	1	6	4	7	2
6	4	2	5	7	8	9	3	1

10

2	4	5	3	8	6	9	7	1
6	7	3	9	2	1	5	8	4
1	8	9	4	7	5	3	2	6
3	2	7	6	4	9	8	1	5
5	1	6	2	3	8	4	9	7
8	9	4	5	1	7	2	6	3
7	5	8	1	9	3	6	4	2
9	6	2	7	5	4	1	3	8
4	3	1	8	6	2	7	5	9

11

4	5	8	2	1	7	6	3	9
9	2	3	6	8	5	1	4	7
6	7	1	4	3	9	5	2	8
5	9	6	3	2	4	7	8	1
8	4	7	9	5	1	3	6	2
1	3	2	8	7	6	9	5	4
3	1	5	7	4	8	2	9	6
2	8	9	1	6	3	4	7	5
7	6	4	5	9	2	8	1	3

12

7	6	3	8	9	2	1	5	4
5	9	1	6	3	4	7	8	2
2	4	8	5	1	7	6	3	9
1	2	7	4	8	5	3	9	6
8	3	4	9	6	1	5	2	7
9	5	6	2	7	3	4	1	8
4	8	9	1	5	6	2	7	3
3	1	2	7	4	9	8	6	5
6	7	5	3	2	8	9	4	1

13

8	2	5	3	6	1	7	9	4
7	1	3	9	2	4	8	5	6
4	6	9	5	7	8	2	3	1
2	9	8	6	4	3	5	1	7
1	3	7	8	5	2	4	6	9
6	5	4	7	1	9	3	2	8
5	7	1	4	3	6	9	8	2
9	4	2	1	8	5	6	7	3
3	8	6	2	9	7	1	4	5

14

9	3	5	1	7	4	2	8	6
2	7	6	3	8	5	9	4	1
1	8	4	9	2	6	3	7	5
6	2	9	7	1	3	4	5	8
4	5	7	6	9	8	1	2	3
3	1	8	4	5	2	6	9	7
7	6	2	8	4	1	5	3	9
5	9	1	2	3	7	8	6	4
8	4	3	5	6	9	7	1	2

15

6	1	7	9	3	5	4	2	8
8	5	2	7	1	4	6	3	9
3	4	9	2	6	8	1	5	7
4	7	5	6	9	1	3	8	2
1	8	3	5	4	2	9	7	6
9	2	6	8	7	3	5	4	1
5	6	4	1	2	7	8	9	3
2	3	1	4	8	9	7	6	5
7	9	8	3	5	6	2	1	4

16

1	8	3	5	9	6	7	2	4
7	6	4	2	3	8	9	5	1
2	5	9	1	4	7	6	8	3
3	4	8	9	2	1	5	7	6
5	7	6	3	8	4	1	9	2
9	2	1	7	6	5	3	4	8
4	9	5	8	1	3	2	6	7
6	1	7	4	5	2	8	3	9
8	3	2	6	7	9	4	1	5

17

4	9	3	6	8	7	5	1	2
7	5	2	3	1	9	4	8	6
8	1	6	2	5	4	9	7	3
9	2	7	8	4	1	3	6	5
3	8	5	7	2	6	1	9	4
6	4	1	9	3	5	7	2	8
5	6	4	1	9	8	2	3	7
1	3	8	5	7	2	6	4	9
2	7	9	4	6	3	8	5	1

18

1	2	7	4	6	9	8	5	3
4	9	3	5	7	8	2	1	6
5	8	6	1	2	3	9	7	4
3	4	8	7	1	6	5	9	2
6	5	1	3	9	2	4	8	7
9	7	2	8	4	5	3	6	1
8	3	4	6	5	1	7	2	9
2	1	5	9	3	7	6	4	8
7	6	9	2	8	4	1	3	5

19

9	1	2	5	8	4	7	3	6
3	8	7	9	6	2	4	5	1
4	5	6	7	3	1	8	2	9
6	4	5	3	9	7	1	8	2
1	3	8	2	4	5	9	6	7
2	7	9	8	1	6	3	4	5
5	9	4	1	2	8	6	7	3
7	6	3	4	5	9	2	1	8
8	2	1	6	7	3	5	9	4

20

3	8	2	9	5	6	1	7	4
1	6	5	4	7	2	9	3	8
7	9	4	1	3	8	6	5	2
8	3	7	6	9	1	4	2	5
4	1	6	3	2	5	8	9	7
5	2	9	7	8	4	3	6	1
9	5	3	8	1	7	2	4	6
2	4	8	5	6	3	7	1	9
6	7	1	2	4	9	5	8	3

21

6	3	7	1	2	5	9	4	8
8	5	4	6	7	9	2	1	3
9	2	1	8	4	3	7	5	6
5	7	6	3	8	1	4	2	9
4	9	2	7	5	6	3	8	1
1	8	3	2	9	4	5	6	7
2	1	5	9	6	7	8	3	4
3	4	9	5	1	8	6	7	2
7	6	8	4	3	2	1	9	5

22

2	9	5	7	6	1	8	4	3
3	7	4	5	9	8	2	1	6
6	1	8	2	3	4	9	5	7
7	4	6	1	5	9	3	8	2
5	8	3	6	4	2	7	9	1
9	2	1	3	8	7	4	6	5
1	5	9	4	7	3	6	2	8
4	6	7	8	2	5	1	3	9
8	3	2	9	1	6	5	7	4

23

9	7	1	5	2	8	3	4	6
4	3	6	9	7	1	2	5	8
5	2	8	3	4	6	7	1	9
6	4	2	1	3	5	8	9	7
8	1	7	4	9	2	5	6	3
3	9	5	8	6	7	1	2	4
7	6	3	2	1	9	4	8	5
2	8	9	7	5	4	6	3	1
1	5	4	6	8	3	9	7	2

24

5	2	8	4	9	3	1	7	6
7	1	9	5	8	6	2	4	3
4	6	3	7	2	1	9	8	5
6	3	7	9	1	2	8	5	4
2	4	5	3	7	8	6	1	9
9	8	1	6	5	4	3	2	7
8	5	4	2	6	9	7	3	1
3	9	2	1	4	7	5	6	8
1	7	6	8	3	5	4	9	2

25

1	5	9	3	8	2	7	4	6
6	3	2	4	7	1	5	8	9
4	7	8	5	9	6	1	2	3
9	4	3	6	2	7	8	5	1
2	1	6	8	5	4	9	3	7
5	8	7	1	3	9	2	6	4
3	9	5	7	4	8	6	1	2
8	2	1	9	6	3	4	7	5
7	6	4	2	1	5	3	9	8

26

5	1	7	3	2	9	8	6	4
9	8	3	5	4	6	2	1	7
2	6	4	1	7	8	9	3	5
3	2	5	4	8	7	1	9	6
7	4	6	9	3	1	5	8	2
1	9	8	6	5	2	7	4	3
6	5	1	2	9	3	4	7	8
4	7	9	8	6	5	3	2	1
8	3	2	7	1	4	6	5	9

27

2	5	3	9	1	4	8	6	7
8	6	4	5	3	7	2	1	9
9	1	7	2	8	6	5	3	4
6	7	2	8	4	1	9	5	3
5	3	8	7	2	9	1	4	6
1	4	9	3	6	5	7	8	2
4	9	5	6	7	8	3	2	1
3	8	6	1	9	2	4	7	5
7	2	1	4	5	3	6	9	8

28

4	7	8	3	5	1	9	6	2
9	2	1	8	6	4	7	5	3
6	3	5	2	9	7	8	4	1
2	4	6	1	8	5	3	7	9
1	9	7	4	2	3	6	8	5
8	5	3	6	7	9	2	1	4
5	6	9	7	4	2	1	3	8
3	8	4	9	1	6	5	2	7
7	1	2	5	3	8	4	9	6

29

3	5	2	6	4	1	9	7	8
4	1	6	7	8	9	5	3	2
8	7	9	3	2	5	4	1	6
9	8	1	2	7	6	3	5	4
6	3	4	5	1	8	2	9	7
7	2	5	9	3	4	6	8	1
5	4	8	1	6	3	7	2	9
1	9	7	4	5	2	8	6	3
2	6	3	8	9	7	1	4	5

30

9	1	7	2	8	6	4	3	5
5	4	3	9	1	7	8	2	6
8	2	6	3	4	5	1	9	7
6	7	8	4	2	1	9	5	3
3	5	4	6	7	9	2	1	8
1	9	2	5	3	8	6	7	4
4	3	1	8	5	2	7	6	9
7	6	5	1	9	4	3	8	2
2	8	9	7	6	3	5	4	1

31

8	5	1	6	4	3	9	7	2
3	7	2	9	1	5	6	4	8
4	9	6	2	7	8	5	3	1
1	4	9	3	8	7	2	6	5
2	8	3	5	6	9	7	1	4
5	6	7	4	2	1	8	9	3
7	3	4	8	5	6	1	2	9
9	1	8	7	3	2	4	5	6
6	2	5	1	9	4	3	8	7

32

1	3	2	4	6	9	7	5	8
5	7	6	3	8	2	9	1	4
8	4	9	1	7	5	2	6	3
2	6	8	5	4	7	3	9	1
9	1	4	2	3	6	5	8	7
3	5	7	9	1	8	4	2	6
4	9	1	8	5	3	6	7	2
7	2	3	6	9	1	8	4	5
6	8	5	7	2	4	1	3	9

33

9	1	5	6	7	3	2	4	8
8	6	2	4	9	1	7	5	3
3	7	4	8	2	5	6	9	1
5	4	6	1	8	2	3	7	9
1	3	9	7	4	6	8	2	5
7	2	8	3	5	9	1	6	4
6	9	3	2	1	4	5	8	7
4	8	1	5	6	7	9	3	2
2	5	7	9	3	8	4	1	6

34

1	2	9	5	8	7	3	6	4
4	5	3	6	1	2	9	7	8
7	6	8	3	4	9	1	5	2
3	1	4	9	6	5	8	2	7
9	7	5	8	2	4	6	1	3
6	8	2	7	3	1	4	9	5
5	3	7	1	9	8	2	4	6
2	9	6	4	5	3	7	8	1
8	4	1	2	7	6	5	3	9

35

3	6	8	4	1	7	9	2	5
5	9	2	3	8	6	1	4	7
1	7	4	5	2	9	3	6	8
9	3	6	7	4	2	5	8	1
4	1	5	8	9	3	2	7	6
2	8	7	6	5	1	4	3	9
6	2	1	9	7	4	8	5	3
7	5	9	2	3	8	6	1	4
8	4	3	1	6	5	7	9	2

36

2	8	7	3	5	4	1	9	6
1	6	3	9	7	8	2	4	5
5	4	9	2	6	1	7	8	3
6	5	4	8	9	2	3	1	7
8	7	1	4	3	5	6	2	9
3	9	2	7	1	6	8	5	4
4	3	5	1	8	7	9	6	2
9	2	8	6	4	3	5	7	1
7	1	6	5	2	9	4	3	8

37

5	7	4	3	6	9	1	2	8
3	1	8	5	2	4	6	9	7
9	2	6	1	7	8	3	5	4
8	9	1	7	3	5	2	4	6
2	4	7	8	1	6	9	3	5
6	5	3	9	4	2	8	7	1
4	6	5	2	9	1	7	8	3
7	8	9	6	5	3	4	1	2
1	3	2	4	8	7	5	6	9

38

4	1	9	3	6	2	8	5	7
3	8	6	5	1	7	4	2	9
5	2	7	9	4	8	6	3	1
7	5	4	2	9	3	1	8	6
8	3	1	4	5	6	9	7	2
6	9	2	7	8	1	3	4	5
2	4	8	6	7	9	5	1	3
9	7	5	1	3	4	2	6	8
1	6	3	8	2	5	7	9	4

39

2	1	8	5	4	6	7	9	3
4	9	3	7	1	8	6	5	2
6	7	5	3	2	9	4	1	8
1	2	4	6	9	5	3	8	7
8	3	6	2	7	1	5	4	9
7	5	9	8	3	4	2	6	1
5	6	2	9	8	7	1	3	4
3	8	1	4	5	2	9	7	6
9	4	7	1	6	3	8	2	5

40

2	4	1	3	8	9	5	6	7
5	3	7	2	1	6	8	4	9
8	6	9	4	5	7	3	1	2
4	5	2	7	3	1	9	8	6
1	7	8	9	6	2	4	3	5
6	9	3	5	4	8	2	7	1
9	8	5	6	7	4	1	2	3
3	1	6	8	2	5	7	9	4
7	2	4	1	9	3	6	5	8

41

3	1	6	7	9	8	2	5	4
2	5	4	1	6	3	8	9	7
7	9	8	5	2	4	1	6	3
1	7	3	8	4	6	5	2	9
5	8	2	3	1	9	7	4	6
6	4	9	2	5	7	3	1	8
4	3	5	6	7	2	9	8	1
9	2	7	4	8	1	6	3	5
8	6	1	9	3	5	4	7	2

42

1	6	3	2	9	4	8	5	7
7	9	8	1	5	6	4	2	3
5	4	2	8	7	3	1	9	6
9	7	6	5	8	1	3	4	2
8	3	4	6	2	9	7	1	5
2	5	1	3	4	7	9	6	8
6	1	7	4	3	5	2	8	9
4	2	9	7	6	8	5	3	1
3	8	5	9	1	2	6	7	4

43

4	7	5	3	8	2	1	6	9
6	1	9	5	7	4	3	2	8
3	8	2	6	9	1	4	5	7
1	6	8	2	3	9	7	4	5
2	5	4	8	6	7	9	1	3
7	9	3	4	1	5	2	8	6
5	3	1	9	4	8	6	7	2
9	2	7	1	5	6	8	3	4
8	4	6	7	2	3	5	9	1

44

3	1	9	7	8	5	2	6	4
2	8	4	1	9	6	7	3	5
7	6	5	3	2	4	8	1	9
4	2	8	5	7	1	3	9	6
6	9	1	2	3	8	5	4	7
5	3	7	6	4	9	1	8	2
8	5	6	4	1	7	9	2	3
9	4	3	8	5	2	6	7	1
1	7	2	9	6	3	4	5	8

45

6	5	3	7	9	4	1	8	2
4	8	2	3	5	1	9	6	7
9	7	1	8	2	6	5	4	3
8	2	4	6	3	9	7	1	5
1	3	7	4	8	5	2	9	6
5	9	6	1	7	2	4	3	8
3	1	8	5	4	7	6	2	9
7	6	9	2	1	3	8	5	4
2	4	5	9	6	8	3	7	1

46

6	3	7	5	8	4	1	9	2
1	5	8	9	2	3	4	6	7
9	4	2	7	1	6	5	8	3
3	8	9	2	7	1	6	5	4
2	6	5	4	3	9	8	7	1
7	1	4	6	5	8	3	2	9
8	2	1	3	9	5	7	4	6
5	9	6	1	4	7	2	3	8
4	7	3	8	6	2	9	1	5

47

5	7	4	2	9	6	3	1	8
9	8	3	5	1	7	4	6	2
2	1	6	4	3	8	9	7	5
4	9	2	8	7	1	5	3	6
8	3	7	6	5	2	1	4	9
6	5	1	3	4	9	8	2	7
7	4	9	1	6	5	2	8	3
3	2	5	7	8	4	6	9	1
1	6	8	9	2	3	7	5	4

48

9	7	1	2	6	5	4	3	8
2	4	5	1	8	3	6	9	7
8	3	6	4	7	9	2	1	5
1	9	8	7	2	4	3	5	6
5	6	4	3	1	8	7	2	9
3	2	7	5	9	6	1	8	4
4	8	3	6	5	2	9	7	1
7	5	2	9	4	1	8	6	3
6	1	9	8	3	7	5	4	2

49

2	1	4	8	5	6	7	9	3
9	7	5	2	4	3	8	6	1
3	8	6	9	7	1	4	2	5
6	3	2	5	8	4	1	7	9
1	5	7	6	9	2	3	8	4
8	4	9	3	1	7	2	5	6
5	9	3	1	2	8	6	4	7
7	6	8	4	3	9	5	1	2
4	2	1	7	6	5	9	3	8

50

6	5	9	2	4	8	3	1	7
1	8	3	9	7	5	2	4	6
4	2	7	6	3	1	8	5	9
9	3	2	5	6	7	1	8	4
5	4	8	1	2	9	7	6	3
7	1	6	3	8	4	9	2	5
8	9	4	7	5	2	6	3	1
2	6	1	4	9	3	5	7	8
3	7	5	8	1	6	4	9	2

51

4	3	1	6	7	5	9	8	2
9	8	2	3	4	1	7	5	6
7	6	5	9	2	8	3	4	1
1	7	6	8	5	4	2	9	3
2	5	9	1	3	7	8	6	4
8	4	3	2	6	9	1	7	5
3	9	7	4	1	6	5	2	8
6	2	8	5	9	3	4	1	7
5	1	4	7	8	2	6	3	9

52

3	2	6	9	5	7	8	1	4
1	9	8	4	2	6	5	7	3
4	5	7	1	8	3	2	9	6
9	3	1	7	6	8	4	2	5
2	8	5	3	4	9	1	6	7
6	7	4	5	1	2	3	8	9
7	1	9	2	3	4	6	5	8
8	4	2	6	9	5	7	3	1
5	6	3	8	7	1	9	4	2

53

8	5	9	4	2	1	6	7	3
4	1	3	5	6	7	9	2	8
6	7	2	9	8	3	5	1	4
1	2	7	3	5	8	4	6	9
5	6	4	7	9	2	3	8	1
3	9	8	6	1	4	2	5	7
9	4	6	1	7	5	8	3	2
7	8	5	2	3	9	1	4	6
2	3	1	8	4	6	7	9	5

54

1	5	8	3	9	7	4	6	2
3	9	6	2	4	8	1	7	5
4	7	2	5	6	1	8	3	9
5	2	3	7	1	4	9	8	6
9	8	4	6	2	5	3	1	7
6	1	7	9	8	3	2	5	4
7	4	5	1	3	2	6	9	8
8	3	9	4	5	6	7	2	1
2	6	1	8	7	9	5	4	3

55

5	7	2	3	6	9	1	8	4
6	8	3	4	1	2	7	9	5
9	4	1	7	5	8	2	3	6
3	1	6	8	2	4	5	7	9
4	5	8	1	9	7	6	2	3
7	2	9	6	3	5	4	1	8
8	3	5	2	7	6	9	4	1
1	6	7	9	4	3	8	5	2
2	9	4	5	8	1	3	6	7

56

7	5	2	8	3	6	4	1	9
3	1	4	9	5	2	8	7	6
8	6	9	7	4	1	5	3	2
1	2	5	3	6	7	9	8	4
9	7	6	4	8	5	1	2	3
4	8	3	1	2	9	7	6	5
5	3	8	2	7	4	6	9	1
2	4	1	6	9	8	3	5	7
6	9	7	5	1	3	2	4	8

57

2	5	1	8	6	3	9	4	7
6	9	7	4	1	5	8	2	3
8	3	4	9	7	2	1	5	6
9	4	6	5	2	7	3	1	8
5	8	3	1	9	6	2	7	4
1	7	2	3	8	4	6	9	5
7	6	8	2	4	1	5	3	9
3	2	9	7	5	8	4	6	1
4	1	5	6	3	9	7	8	2

58

1	6	7	3	5	8	2	9	4
8	2	5	9	1	4	3	7	6
4	9	3	7	2	6	1	8	5
3	5	4	6	9	1	8	2	7
2	7	6	8	4	3	5	1	9
9	1	8	5	7	2	6	4	3
6	3	9	1	8	7	4	5	2
5	4	1	2	6	9	7	3	8
7	8	2	4	3	5	9	6	1

59

6	2	4	8	7	5	1	3	9
5	9	1	4	3	2	7	8	6
8	7	3	1	6	9	4	5	2
2	8	6	7	9	1	3	4	5
7	3	5	2	4	6	9	1	8
1	4	9	5	8	3	6	2	7
9	1	8	3	5	7	2	6	4
4	6	2	9	1	8	5	7	3
3	5	7	6	2	4	8	9	1

60

2	1	9	4	6	8	3	7	5
4	7	3	1	9	5	2	6	8
8	6	5	3	7	2	9	4	1
3	4	6	5	2	7	8	1	9
1	8	2	9	4	3	6	5	7
9	5	7	8	1	6	4	2	3
5	9	4	2	8	1	7	3	6
6	3	8	7	5	4	1	9	2
7	2	1	6	3	9	5	8	4

61

5	3	7	1	6	2	4	8	9
9	4	2	7	5	8	6	1	3
8	6	1	4	9	3	7	5	2
6	1	9	2	8	4	3	7	5
4	7	5	3	1	9	2	6	8
3	2	8	6	7	5	1	9	4
7	9	3	8	2	1	5	4	6
2	8	6	5	4	7	9	3	1
1	5	4	9	3	6	8	2	7

62

8	9	6	5	1	2	7	4	3
4	1	3	7	9	8	5	6	2
2	5	7	4	3	6	8	9	1
3	4	9	8	2	5	6	1	7
7	6	8	1	4	9	3	2	5
5	2	1	6	7	3	4	8	9
1	3	5	9	8	4	2	7	6
9	8	2	3	6	7	1	5	4
6	7	4	2	5	1	9	3	8

63

9	2	7	6	4	1	5	8	3
8	5	6	2	9	3	4	1	7
3	4	1	7	8	5	9	6	2
5	8	2	1	3	9	6	7	4
7	3	4	5	2	6	1	9	8
6	1	9	4	7	8	3	2	5
2	9	5	3	1	7	8	4	6
4	6	8	9	5	2	7	3	1
1	7	3	8	6	4	2	5	9

64

7	4	9	6	1	5	8	2	3
8	5	2	3	4	9	6	1	7
6	3	1	8	2	7	5	9	4
9	2	6	4	7	1	3	5	8
1	8	5	9	6	3	4	7	2
4	7	3	5	8	2	1	6	9
5	1	8	7	9	4	2	3	6
2	6	7	1	3	8	9	4	5
3	9	4	2	5	6	7	8	1

65

7	5	1	8	6	4	9	3	2
2	9	4	3	5	1	6	7	8
6	3	8	9	2	7	5	1	4
5	1	2	4	3	9	8	6	7
8	6	9	7	1	2	4	5	3
3	4	7	5	8	6	2	9	1
1	2	5	6	7	8	3	4	9
4	8	6	1	9	3	7	2	5
9	7	3	2	4	5	1	8	6

66

8	3	7	1	6	9	2	5	4
9	2	6	5	3	4	8	1	7
4	1	5	7	8	2	3	9	6
2	7	1	3	4	5	6	8	9
3	6	9	8	7	1	5	4	2
5	8	4	2	9	6	7	3	1
6	4	3	9	5	7	1	2	8
7	5	2	4	1	8	9	6	3
1	9	8	6	2	3	4	7	5

67

5	3	8	4	6	2	7	1	9
2	1	4	9	5	7	6	3	8
7	9	6	1	3	8	2	5	4
1	8	5	7	9	3	4	2	6
3	2	9	6	8	4	1	7	5
4	6	7	2	1	5	8	9	3
6	4	3	5	2	1	9	8	7
9	5	2	8	7	6	3	4	1
8	7	1	3	4	9	5	6	2

68

4	5	8	9	1	7	6	2	3
2	9	1	6	5	3	7	8	4
6	7	3	4	2	8	9	1	5
3	4	7	8	6	2	1	5	9
9	6	5	1	7	4	2	3	8
8	1	2	3	9	5	4	7	6
1	8	6	2	3	9	5	4	7
7	3	9	5	4	1	8	6	2
5	2	4	7	8	6	3	9	1

69

3	8	4	2	7	1	9	5	6
9	2	7	6	5	4	1	8	3
5	6	1	8	3	9	2	7	4
1	9	6	7	2	5	4	3	8
7	4	8	1	6	3	5	2	9
2	3	5	9	4	8	6	1	7
8	5	9	3	1	6	7	4	2
4	7	3	5	9	2	8	6	1
6	1	2	4	8	7	3	9	5

70

6	1	2	9	4	8	5	7	3
3	5	9	1	7	6	4	2	8
7	8	4	3	5	2	1	9	6
1	7	5	4	9	3	8	6	2
9	2	3	6	8	5	7	1	4
8	4	6	7	2	1	3	5	9
4	9	8	5	6	7	2	3	1
5	6	1	2	3	4	9	8	7
2	3	7	8	1	9	6	4	5

71

8	2	3	9	4	6	5	7	1
5	1	4	7	8	2	3	6	9
6	9	7	5	1	3	2	8	4
9	5	2	1	3	8	6	4	7
4	7	1	2	6	9	8	3	5
3	6	8	4	7	5	1	9	2
1	4	6	3	2	7	9	5	8
2	8	9	6	5	4	7	1	3
7	3	5	8	9	1	4	2	6

72

8	3	9	5	4	1	7	2	6
5	6	2	3	9	7	4	8	1
1	4	7	8	6	2	3	9	5
9	7	4	1	8	6	2	5	3
3	2	1	9	5	4	8	6	7
6	5	8	7	2	3	9	1	4
2	1	5	4	7	9	6	3	8
7	8	6	2	3	5	1	4	9
4	9	3	6	1	8	5	7	2

73

1	2	3	5	6	9	8	7	4
5	4	7	8	3	1	6	2	9
9	8	6	4	2	7	5	3	1
6	5	4	9	8	3	7	1	2
3	7	1	6	5	2	9	4	8
2	9	8	7	1	4	3	6	5
8	3	2	1	9	6	4	5	7
4	6	5	2	7	8	1	9	3
7	1	9	3	4	5	2	8	6

74

5	6	9	2	1	3	8	4	7
7	8	3	4	9	6	5	2	1
4	1	2	5	7	8	3	6	9
9	3	1	6	2	4	7	8	5
2	4	8	1	5	7	9	3	6
6	7	5	8	3	9	4	1	2
3	9	6	7	4	2	1	5	8
8	5	4	9	6	1	2	7	3
1	2	7	3	8	5	6	9	4

75

3	1	2	5	6	7	8	9	4
9	8	6	2	3	4	5	1	7
7	4	5	1	9	8	3	6	2
5	7	1	4	8	6	9	2	3
4	2	9	3	1	5	7	8	6
8	6	3	7	2	9	4	5	1
2	3	8	9	7	1	6	4	5
6	5	7	8	4	2	1	3	9
1	9	4	6	5	3	2	7	8

76

5	4	7	8	2	6	3	1	9
3	1	9	7	4	5	2	8	6
2	8	6	3	9	1	7	4	5
1	3	2	9	6	4	5	7	8
7	9	8	5	3	2	1	6	4
6	5	4	1	7	8	9	3	2
8	2	1	6	5	7	4	9	3
4	7	3	2	8	9	6	5	1
9	6	5	4	1	3	8	2	7

77

7	3	2	9	4	8	1	5	6
9	8	5	6	1	7	4	2	3
1	4	6	5	2	3	8	9	7
2	6	8	7	3	1	5	4	9
3	5	7	4	8	9	6	1	2
4	9	1	2	5	6	7	3	8
6	7	3	1	9	4	2	8	5
8	2	4	3	6	5	9	7	1
5	1	9	8	7	2	3	6	4

78

8	5	6	1	2	7	9	4	3
4	2	9	5	6	3	8	7	1
1	3	7	9	4	8	5	6	2
5	9	8	6	7	1	3	2	4
2	1	4	8	3	5	7	9	6
7	6	3	4	9	2	1	5	8
9	7	1	2	8	6	4	3	5
3	8	2	7	5	4	6	1	9
6	4	5	3	1	9	2	8	7

79

7	2	3	5	6	1	8	4	9
5	1	4	8	9	2	3	6	7
8	9	6	4	3	7	5	2	1
1	8	7	9	5	4	6	3	2
3	5	2	6	7	8	1	9	4
6	4	9	2	1	3	7	8	5
2	6	1	7	8	9	4	5	3
9	3	5	1	4	6	2	7	8
4	7	8	3	2	5	9	1	6

80

2	3	1	4	9	8	7	5	6
6	9	5	2	7	3	4	8	1
4	7	8	1	5	6	9	3	2
1	6	7	8	2	4	5	9	3
5	8	9	3	6	7	1	2	4
3	2	4	5	1	9	8	6	7
7	5	6	9	4	2	3	1	8
8	1	2	7	3	5	6	4	9
9	4	3	6	8	1	2	7	5

81

9	5	8	2	7	6	3	1	4
3	4	2	1	5	9	6	7	8
7	1	6	4	8	3	9	2	5
1	6	3	7	9	5	4	8	2
5	8	7	3	4	2	1	9	6
4	2	9	8	6	1	5	3	7
6	3	1	5	2	7	8	4	9
2	9	4	6	1	8	7	5	3
8	7	5	9	3	4	2	6	1

82

1	4	2	5	9	3	7	8	6
3	7	8	6	2	4	5	1	9
6	5	9	8	7	1	4	3	2
9	6	7	2	3	5	8	4	1
4	1	3	7	8	6	9	2	5
8	2	5	4	1	9	3	6	7
7	8	4	1	5	2	6	9	3
2	3	6	9	4	7	1	5	8
5	9	1	3	6	8	2	7	4

83

6	8	7	1	9	2	3	5	4
4	5	9	7	3	6	2	8	1
3	2	1	5	8	4	9	7	6
7	4	8	6	1	3	5	9	2
9	6	2	8	7	5	1	4	3
1	3	5	2	4	9	8	6	7
5	1	6	4	2	8	7	3	9
2	9	4	3	5	7	6	1	8
8	7	3	9	6	1	4	2	5

84

1	8	7	3	2	9	5	4	6
3	9	6	4	5	1	7	2	8
4	2	5	7	6	8	1	3	9
9	1	4	8	7	2	6	5	3
5	7	8	9	3	6	2	1	4
2	6	3	1	4	5	9	8	7
8	5	9	6	1	4	3	7	2
7	4	2	5	9	3	8	6	1
6	3	1	2	8	7	4	9	5

85

4	3	7	6	9	8	5	2	1
9	8	5	3	2	1	4	7	6
1	2	6	5	7	4	8	3	9
8	4	3	1	6	5	2	9	7
6	7	9	2	4	3	1	5	8
2	5	1	9	8	7	6	4	3
3	9	2	8	5	6	7	1	4
7	1	8	4	3	2	9	6	5
5	6	4	7	1	9	3	8	2

86

5	2	7	6	8	3	1	9	4
9	8	1	2	4	7	5	3	6
4	3	6	1	9	5	8	2	7
2	4	5	7	3	1	9	6	8
1	7	3	9	6	8	4	5	2
6	9	8	5	2	4	3	7	1
8	6	4	3	7	9	2	1	5
3	5	2	4	1	6	7	8	9
7	1	9	8	5	2	6	4	3

87

3	6	2	1	4	9	5	7	8
7	5	8	2	3	6	4	9	1
4	9	1	8	5	7	3	6	2
5	3	7	9	1	2	8	4	6
6	8	4	3	7	5	2	1	9
1	2	9	6	8	4	7	3	5
8	7	5	4	6	1	9	2	3
9	1	3	7	2	8	6	5	4
2	4	6	5	9	3	1	8	7

88

3	2	6	8	9	4	1	7	5
9	7	1	2	3	5	6	4	8
4	5	8	7	1	6	2	3	9
1	6	3	5	2	7	9	8	4
5	9	4	6	8	3	7	2	1
7	8	2	1	4	9	5	6	3
6	4	5	3	7	1	8	9	2
2	3	7	9	5	8	4	1	6
8	1	9	4	6	2	3	5	7

89

6	7	5	3	2	8	1	9	4
4	9	1	6	5	7	2	8	3
8	2	3	4	9	1	7	6	5
3	6	2	5	1	4	8	7	9
9	8	7	2	6	3	4	5	1
5	1	4	8	7	9	3	2	6
1	3	9	7	8	5	6	4	2
2	5	8	1	4	6	9	3	7
7	4	6	9	3	2	5	1	8

90

7	8	5	2	3	4	1	9	6
1	9	3	5	8	6	7	4	2
4	2	6	7	9	1	5	8	3
8	1	7	9	2	5	3	6	4
6	4	2	3	1	8	9	5	7
5	3	9	4	6	7	8	2	1
3	5	4	8	7	2	6	1	9
9	6	8	1	4	3	2	7	5
2	7	1	6	5	9	4	3	8

91

4	8	1	9	6	7	5	3	2
5	2	7	4	3	8	1	6	9
3	9	6	2	1	5	7	4	8
2	7	8	5	9	4	6	1	3
6	1	4	8	2	3	9	7	5
9	5	3	1	7	6	2	8	4
7	4	5	6	8	9	3	2	1
1	6	9	3	4	2	8	5	7
8	3	2	7	5	1	4	9	6

92

3	4	5	2	8	6	1	9	7
7	6	1	9	4	5	8	3	2
9	8	2	1	3	7	4	6	5
1	3	6	8	7	9	5	2	4
4	9	7	3	5	2	6	8	1
2	5	8	6	1	4	9	7	3
5	7	9	4	2	8	3	1	6
6	2	3	5	9	1	7	4	8
8	1	4	7	6	3	2	5	9

93

8	4	7	9	5	6	3	1	2
9	2	1	8	4	3	5	7	6
6	5	3	2	1	7	4	8	9
1	9	5	4	6	2	7	3	8
3	7	4	5	8	9	2	6	1
2	8	6	3	7	1	9	5	4
7	6	2	1	3	4	8	9	5
4	1	8	7	9	5	6	2	3
5	3	9	6	2	8	1	4	7

94

3	4	5	1	6	2	8	7	9
7	8	2	4	5	9	1	3	6
1	6	9	8	7	3	5	4	2
6	9	4	7	8	1	2	5	3
5	3	7	9	2	4	6	1	8
8	2	1	5	3	6	4	9	7
9	5	8	2	4	7	3	6	1
4	1	3	6	9	8	7	2	5
2	7	6	3	1	5	9	8	4

95

8	9	2	6	1	5	3	4	7
6	1	7	4	8	3	2	9	5
5	3	4	2	7	9	1	6	8
2	4	8	5	3	7	6	1	9
9	6	1	8	4	2	7	5	3
7	5	3	1	9	6	4	8	2
1	2	5	7	6	8	9	3	4
3	7	6	9	5	4	8	2	1
4	8	9	3	2	1	5	7	6

96

1	8	9	5	6	2	4	3	7
3	6	7	9	1	4	2	5	8
2	4	5	8	3	7	1	6	9
9	7	3	2	8	1	5	4	6
6	2	8	4	7	5	3	9	1
5	1	4	3	9	6	7	8	2
4	5	6	7	2	8	9	1	3
7	3	1	6	5	9	8	2	4
8	9	2	1	4	3	6	7	5

97

2	1	3	5	8	9	4	7	6
7	9	6	3	2	4	1	5	8
5	8	4	6	7	1	2	9	3
3	2	7	8	1	5	9	6	4
4	6	8	7	9	3	5	1	2
9	5	1	2	4	6	3	8	7
8	3	5	1	6	2	7	4	9
6	4	2	9	5	7	8	3	1
1	7	9	4	3	8	6	2	5

98

8	2	4	7	3	9	6	1	5
9	6	5	4	2	1	8	7	3
7	3	1	8	6	5	9	2	4
6	9	2	5	7	4	3	8	1
1	5	3	6	8	2	4	9	7
4	8	7	9	1	3	5	6	2
5	1	6	3	9	7	2	4	8
2	4	8	1	5	6	7	3	9
3	7	9	2	4	8	1	5	6

99

4	1	5	8	2	6	9	3	7
2	9	6	7	3	5	4	8	1
7	3	8	9	1	4	6	5	2
1	7	9	2	5	3	8	4	6
8	5	4	1	6	7	2	9	3
6	2	3	4	8	9	1	7	5
5	6	2	3	4	8	7	1	9
9	8	1	5	7	2	3	6	4
3	4	7	6	9	1	5	2	8

100

1	5	4	2	3	7	8	6	9
7	6	8	1	9	5	4	2	3
3	9	2	6	8	4	7	1	5
2	4	5	3	1	9	6	7	8
8	1	3	7	6	2	5	9	4
6	7	9	5	4	8	1	3	2
4	3	6	8	2	1	9	5	7
9	2	7	4	5	6	3	8	1
5	8	1	9	7	3	2	4	6

101

4	5	9	1	6	7	8	2	3
7	3	8	4	2	9	6	5	1
1	6	2	3	5	8	4	7	9
6	9	7	8	1	2	5	3	4
5	2	1	9	3	4	7	6	8
8	4	3	6	7	5	9	1	2
2	8	5	7	9	3	1	4	6
9	7	6	2	4	1	3	8	5
3	1	4	5	8	6	2	9	7

102

9	3	6	7	5	4	2	8	1
5	4	7	1	8	2	3	9	6
8	1	2	9	6	3	4	7	5
4	2	3	6	7	9	1	5	8
1	9	5	3	2	8	6	4	7
6	7	8	4	1	5	9	3	2
3	8	1	2	9	7	5	6	4
7	6	4	5	3	1	8	2	9
2	5	9	8	4	6	7	1	3

103

7	8	5	2	4	6	9	1	3
1	9	4	7	3	8	6	5	2
6	2	3	1	5	9	7	4	8
8	5	7	4	1	3	2	9	6
9	4	6	8	7	2	1	3	5
2	3	1	9	6	5	4	8	7
4	6	8	3	2	1	5	7	9
5	7	9	6	8	4	3	2	1
3	1	2	5	9	7	8	6	4

104

8	1	5	2	7	6	3	9	4
7	3	9	1	4	8	5	6	2
6	2	4	3	9	5	8	7	1
4	9	2	8	1	7	6	3	5
5	8	6	4	2	3	7	1	9
1	7	3	5	6	9	4	2	8
9	5	7	6	8	2	1	4	3
3	6	1	9	5	4	2	8	7
2	4	8	7	3	1	9	5	6

105

5	3	2	1	6	4	8	7	9
4	7	1	8	3	9	2	6	5
8	9	6	7	5	2	1	3	4
7	6	8	9	1	5	4	2	3
3	4	9	2	7	6	5	8	1
2	1	5	3	4	8	6	9	7
6	2	4	5	9	7	3	1	8
9	8	3	4	2	1	7	5	6
1	5	7	6	8	3	9	4	2

106

8	5	6	7	4	1	3	9	2
9	3	2	5	6	8	1	7	4
1	7	4	3	9	2	5	6	8
3	2	7	6	8	4	9	1	5
4	9	1	2	5	7	8	3	6
5	6	8	1	3	9	2	4	7
6	8	5	9	7	3	4	2	1
2	4	3	8	1	6	7	5	9
7	1	9	4	2	5	6	8	3

107

9	6	3	2	4	1	7	8	5
8	5	1	9	6	7	3	4	2
7	2	4	5	8	3	6	9	1
6	7	2	8	3	9	1	5	4
3	4	5	1	2	6	9	7	8
1	9	8	7	5	4	2	6	3
2	1	6	4	9	5	8	3	7
5	3	7	6	1	8	4	2	9
4	8	9	3	7	2	5	1	6

108

5	8	2	1	7	4	3	6	9
4	9	1	6	3	2	8	7	5
7	6	3	8	9	5	2	1	4
6	1	7	5	4	8	9	2	3
9	3	5	7	2	6	4	8	1
8	2	4	9	1	3	6	5	7
1	5	8	4	6	9	7	3	2
3	7	9	2	8	1	5	4	6
2	4	6	3	5	7	1	9	8

109

5	8	6	7	1	3	2	9	4
2	1	4	9	8	6	5	7	3
3	7	9	5	2	4	8	6	1
4	3	8	1	9	2	7	5	6
6	9	7	4	3	5	1	2	8
1	2	5	6	7	8	4	3	9
7	5	1	8	6	9	3	4	2
9	4	2	3	5	1	6	8	7
8	6	3	2	4	7	9	1	5

110

9	5	8	7	6	1	2	3	4
3	6	7	5	4	2	9	1	8
1	4	2	3	8	9	7	6	5
8	3	5	6	7	4	1	9	2
2	7	9	8	1	5	3	4	6
4	1	6	2	9	3	5	8	7
7	2	4	1	3	8	6	5	9
6	9	1	4	5	7	8	2	3
5	8	3	9	2	6	4	7	1

111

8	3	9	2	6	4	7	1	5
7	5	1	3	9	8	2	4	6
6	2	4	7	1	5	9	3	8
3	8	6	4	5	9	1	7	2
5	4	7	1	2	6	3	8	9
1	9	2	8	3	7	5	6	4
9	7	5	6	4	3	8	2	1
2	6	3	5	8	1	4	9	7
4	1	8	9	7	2	6	5	3

112

4	2	7	9	8	1	6	5	3
6	1	3	4	7	5	8	9	2
5	9	8	6	2	3	7	4	1
7	4	2	1	9	6	3	8	5
1	8	5	2	3	4	9	7	6
3	6	9	7	5	8	2	1	4
8	5	1	3	6	7	4	2	9
9	3	4	8	1	2	5	6	7
2	7	6	5	4	9	1	3	8

113

4	6	3	8	9	5	7	1	2
2	5	7	6	1	3	4	8	9
8	1	9	4	7	2	6	3	5
1	2	6	5	8	9	3	7	4
7	8	4	2	3	1	5	9	6
3	9	5	7	6	4	8	2	1
6	3	2	1	4	8	9	5	7
5	7	8	9	2	6	1	4	3
9	4	1	3	5	7	2	6	8

114

5	4	1	9	8	7	6	2	3
2	7	9	1	3	6	4	8	5
3	6	8	5	2	4	7	1	9
7	8	3	2	5	9	1	6	4
9	1	6	4	7	8	5	3	2
4	2	5	3	6	1	9	7	8
8	3	7	6	9	5	2	4	1
1	9	2	7	4	3	8	5	6
6	5	4	8	1	2	3	9	7

115

9	6	7	4	5	8	2	1	3
1	5	3	9	2	6	4	7	8
4	8	2	1	7	3	5	6	9
5	3	9	2	1	4	6	8	7
2	1	6	7	8	9	3	5	4
8	7	4	6	3	5	9	2	1
6	4	1	5	9	7	8	3	2
3	2	5	8	4	1	7	9	6
7	9	8	3	6	2	1	4	5

116

8	1	7	2	6	3	5	9	4
6	3	9	4	5	1	7	8	2
2	5	4	8	7	9	6	1	3
7	4	1	3	2	6	8	5	9
9	8	2	5	1	4	3	6	7
3	6	5	9	8	7	4	2	1
5	7	8	1	4	2	9	3	6
1	9	6	7	3	5	2	4	8
4	2	3	6	9	8	1	7	5

117

7	3	5	1	2	8	6	9	4
1	6	8	3	9	4	7	2	5
2	4	9	5	6	7	3	8	1
3	2	4	7	8	1	5	6	9
9	8	7	6	4	5	1	3	2
5	1	6	9	3	2	8	4	7
4	7	3	8	1	9	2	5	6
6	9	1	2	5	3	4	7	8
8	5	2	4	7	6	9	1	3

118

2	3	7	9	5	6	8	1	4
6	8	4	7	2	1	5	3	9
5	1	9	3	4	8	7	6	2
8	9	5	6	3	2	4	7	1
3	4	1	5	9	7	2	8	6
7	6	2	8	1	4	9	5	3
1	7	3	2	8	9	6	4	5
9	5	6	4	7	3	1	2	8
4	2	8	1	6	5	3	9	7

119

6	8	1	4	3	7	9	5	2
7	9	2	5	8	6	1	4	3
4	3	5	9	1	2	6	7	8
5	2	3	1	6	4	8	9	7
8	4	9	7	5	3	2	1	6
1	6	7	2	9	8	5	3	4
2	5	4	6	7	9	3	8	1
3	1	6	8	4	5	7	2	9
9	7	8	3	2	1	4	6	5

120

5	6	1	8	2	3	9	4	7
2	8	3	7	4	9	6	1	5
4	7	9	5	6	1	8	2	3
6	9	2	3	5	7	1	8	4
1	4	5	9	8	6	7	3	2
8	3	7	2	1	4	5	9	6
3	1	4	6	7	8	2	5	9
9	5	6	1	3	2	4	7	8
7	2	8	4	9	5	3	6	1

121

2	6	7	5	3	9	8	4	1
4	5	1	2	7	8	6	3	9
8	9	3	1	4	6	7	2	5
5	3	2	7	9	1	4	6	8
1	8	6	4	5	2	9	7	3
7	4	9	8	6	3	5	1	2
6	1	8	9	2	4	3	5	7
3	2	5	6	8	7	1	9	4
9	7	4	3	1	5	2	8	6

122

9	3	2	6	4	8	5	7	1
7	8	5	9	3	1	6	2	4
1	4	6	5	7	2	8	3	9
6	7	9	8	1	4	3	5	2
5	1	3	2	9	6	4	8	7
4	2	8	3	5	7	9	1	6
3	5	7	4	2	9	1	6	8
8	9	1	7	6	5	2	4	3
2	6	4	1	8	3	7	9	5

123

4	2	3	6	1	5	8	7	9
1	8	7	9	4	2	6	3	5
9	6	5	8	7	3	2	4	1
3	9	4	1	2	7	5	6	8
8	1	6	3	5	9	7	2	4
5	7	2	4	6	8	9	1	3
7	3	8	2	9	4	1	5	6
2	4	1	5	8	6	3	9	7
6	5	9	7	3	1	4	8	2

124

2	7	4	1	8	3	9	6	5
9	6	8	5	7	4	1	3	2
1	5	3	2	6	9	4	8	7
8	3	2	9	4	5	6	7	1
6	9	1	3	2	7	5	4	8
5	4	7	8	1	6	2	9	3
7	8	9	4	5	2	3	1	6
4	1	5	6	3	8	7	2	9
3	2	6	7	9	1	8	5	4

125

7	1	9	6	5	8	2	3	4
8	2	4	3	9	1	6	5	7
6	5	3	2	4	7	8	1	9
4	9	8	1	3	6	7	2	5
2	7	5	9	8	4	3	6	1
3	6	1	7	2	5	4	9	8
5	3	7	8	6	9	1	4	2
1	4	6	5	7	2	9	8	3
9	8	2	4	1	3	5	7	6

126

3	8	9	2	4	7	1	6	5
2	6	7	5	1	3	8	9	4
1	5	4	9	6	8	2	3	7
4	9	3	6	8	2	7	5	1
5	2	1	4	7	9	6	8	3
6	7	8	3	5	1	9	4	2
7	3	6	1	9	5	4	2	8
8	4	2	7	3	6	5	1	9
9	1	5	8	2	4	3	7	6

127

3	8	7	9	2	6	4	1	5
5	4	6	8	1	3	9	7	2
1	9	2	4	7	5	8	3	6
2	3	5	7	4	9	1	6	8
9	6	1	2	5	8	7	4	3
4	7	8	6	3	1	5	2	9
7	5	4	3	8	2	6	9	1
6	1	3	5	9	7	2	8	4
8	2	9	1	6	4	3	5	7

128

4	9	1	3	6	7	8	5	2
6	5	2	8	9	4	1	7	3
8	3	7	1	2	5	4	6	9
9	4	5	2	7	8	3	1	6
3	1	8	6	5	9	2	4	7
7	2	6	4	3	1	9	8	5
5	6	4	9	1	2	7	3	8
2	8	3	7	4	6	5	9	1
1	7	9	5	8	3	6	2	4

129

1	8	3	6	4	7	5	9	2
4	9	6	2	3	5	1	8	7
7	5	2	1	8	9	6	4	3
9	6	1	4	2	3	8	7	5
3	7	8	5	1	6	4	2	9
5	2	4	9	7	8	3	1	6
2	4	5	3	9	1	7	6	8
6	1	7	8	5	2	9	3	4
8	3	9	7	6	4	2	5	1

130

3	4	5	9	6	7	1	8	2
2	8	6	1	5	3	9	7	4
7	1	9	8	2	4	6	3	5
9	6	1	3	7	2	5	4	8
5	2	3	4	8	9	7	1	6
4	7	8	5	1	6	3	2	9
8	9	7	2	3	5	4	6	1
6	5	2	7	4	1	8	9	3
1	3	4	6	9	8	2	5	7

131

1	8	4	3	9	6	7	2	5
7	9	2	4	1	5	3	8	6
6	3	5	7	8	2	1	4	9
9	2	7	5	3	8	4	6	1
3	6	1	9	2	4	5	7	8
4	5	8	6	7	1	9	3	2
2	1	9	8	4	3	6	5	7
5	7	3	2	6	9	8	1	4
8	4	6	1	5	7	2	9	3

132

8	6	5	2	1	9	4	3	7
7	1	9	3	4	6	2	8	5
3	2	4	8	7	5	1	9	6
5	9	7	6	8	1	3	2	4
6	3	1	7	2	4	8	5	9
2	4	8	9	5	3	6	7	1
1	7	6	5	3	2	9	4	8
4	5	3	1	9	8	7	6	2
9	8	2	4	6	7	5	1	3

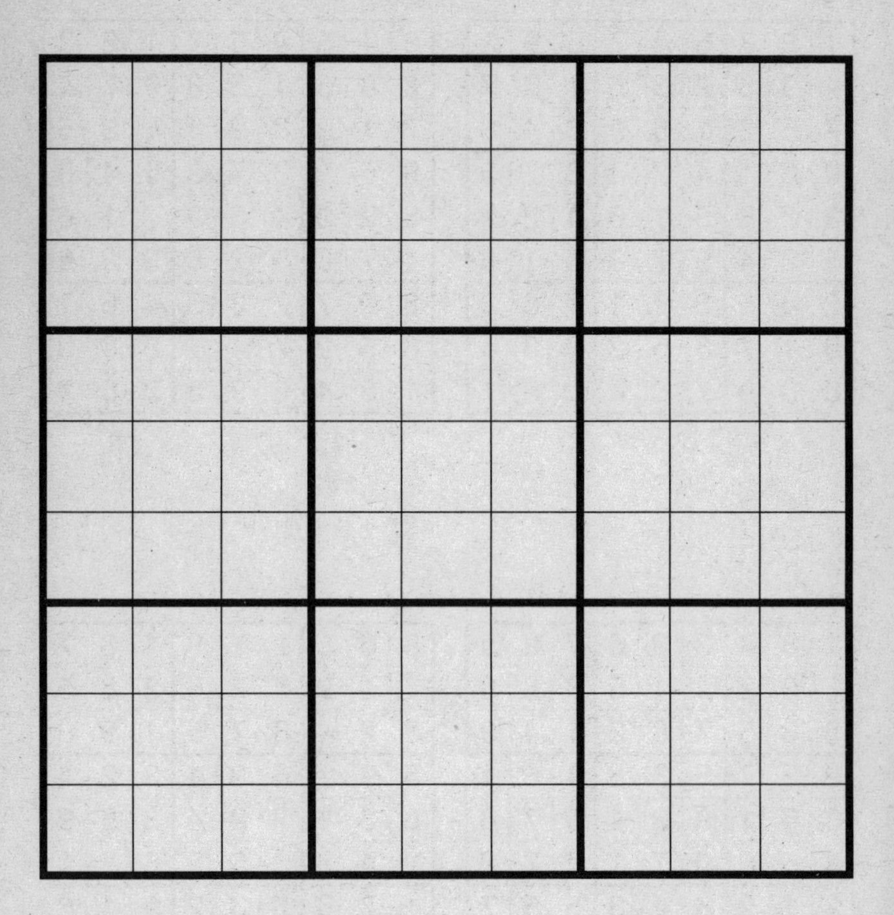

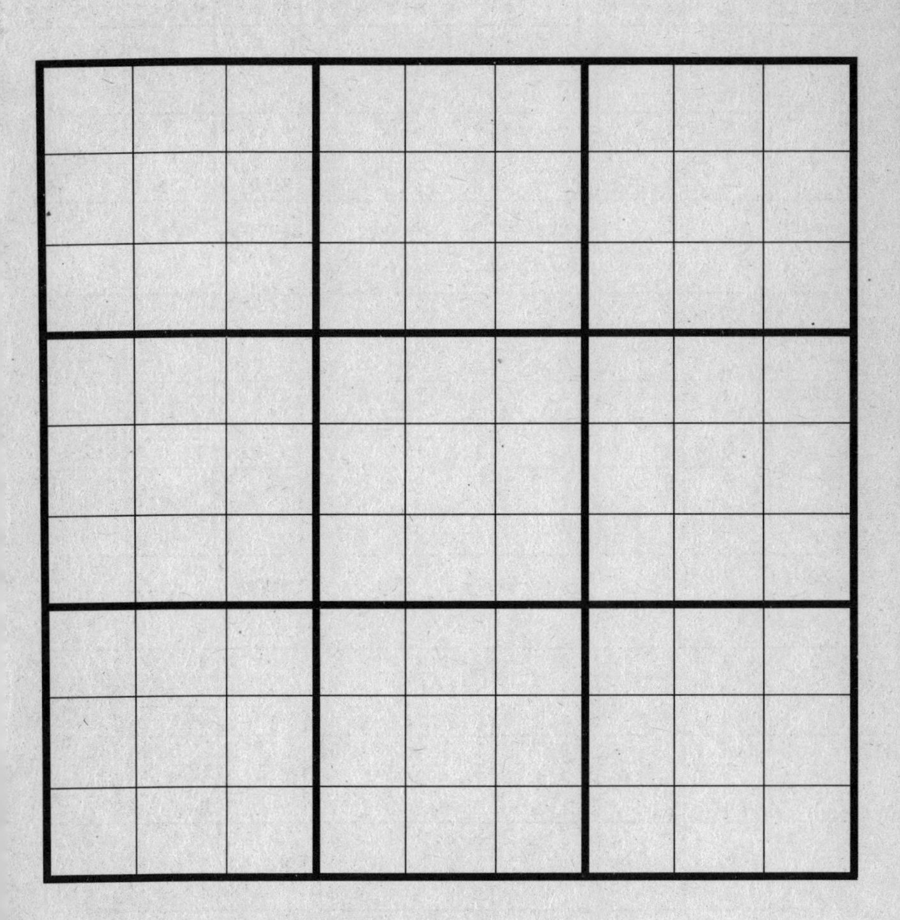

2	5	4	7	3	8	6	1	9
1	9	6	5	4	2	3	8	7
8	7	3	9	6	1	4	2	5
9	6	1	4	2	5	8	7	3
7	3	8	6	1	9	2	5	4
5	4	2	3	8	7	1	9	6
3	8	7	1	9	6	5	4	2
4	2	5	8	7	3	9	6	1
6	1	9	2	5	4	7	3	8

Layer 1

3	8	7	1	9	6	5	4	2
4	2	5	8	7	3	9	6	1
6	1	9	2	5	4	7	3	8
2	5	4	7	3	8	6	1	9
1	9	6	5	4	2	3	8	7
8	7	3	9	6	1	4	2	5
9	6	1	4	2	5	8	7	3
7	3	8	6	1	9	2	5	4
5	4	2	3	8	7	1	9	6

Layer 2

9	6	1	4	2	5	8	7	3
7	3	8	6	1	9	2	5	4
5	4	2	3	8	7	1	9	6
3	8	7	1	9	6	5	4	2
4	2	5	8	7	3	9	6	1
6	1	9	2	5	4	7	3	8
2	5	4	7	3	8	6	1	9
1	9	6	5	4	2	3	8	7
8	7	3	9	6	1	4	2	5

Layer 3

1	9	6	5	4	2	3	8	7
8	7	3	9	6	1	4	2	5
2	5	4	7	3	8	6	1	9
7	3	8	6	1	9	2	5	4
5	4	2	3	8	7	1	9	6
9	6	1	4	2	5	8	7	3
4	2	5	8	7	3	9	6	1
6	1	9	2	5	4	7	3	8
3	8	7	1	9	6	5	4	2

Layer 4

4	2	5	8	7	3	9	6	1
6	1	9	2	5	4	7	3	8
3	8	7	1	9	6	5	4	2
1	9	6	5	4	2	3	8	7
8	7	3	9	6	1	4	2	5
2	5	4	7	3	8	6	1	9
7	3	8	6	1	9	2	5	4
5	4	2	3	8	7	1	9	6
9	6	1	4	2	5	8	7	3

Layer 5

7	3	8	6	1	9	2	5	4
5	4	2	3	8	7	1	9	6
9	6	1	4	2	5	8	7	3
4	2	5	8	7	3	9	6	1
6	1	9	2	5	4	7	3	8
3	8	7	1	9	6	5	4	2
1	9	6	5	4	2	3	8	7
8	7	3	9	6	1	4	2	5
2	5	4	7	3	8	6	1	9

Layer 6

8	7	3	9	6	1	4	2	5
2	5	4	7	3	8	6	1	9
1	9	6	5	4	2	3	8	7
5	4	2	3	8	7	1	9	6
9	6	1	4	2	5	8	7	3
7	3	8	6	1	9	2	5	4
6	1	9	2	5	4	7	3	8
3	8	7	1	9	6	5	4	2
4	2	5	8	7	3	9	6	1

Layer 7

6	1	9	2	5	4	7	3	8
3	8	7	1	9	6	5	4	2
4	2	5	8	7	3	9	6	1
8	7	3	9	6	1	4	2	5
2	5	4	7	3	8	6	1	9
1	9	6	5	4	2	3	8	7
5	4	2	3	8	7	1	9	6
9	6	1	4	2	5	8	7	3
7	3	8	6	1	9	2	5	4

Layer 8

5	4	2	3	8	7	1	9	6
9	6	1	4	2	5	8	7	3
7	3	8	6	1	9	2	5	4
6	1	9	2	5	4	7	3	8
3	8	7	1	9	6	5	4	2
4	2	5	8	7	3	9	6	1
8	7	3	9	6	1	4	2	5
2	5	4	7	3	8	6	1	9
1	9	6	5	4	2	3	8	7

Layer 9